The Manager's Role as Coach

2nd Edition

A Coach Guidebook

Edited by
National Press Publications

National Press Publications, Inc.

A Division of Rockhurst University Continuing Education Center, Inc.
6901 West 63rd St. • P.O. Box 2949 • Shawnee Mission, KS 66201-1349
1-800-258-7246 • 1-913-432-7757

National Press Publications endorses nonsexist language. In an effort to make this handbook clear, consistent and easy to read, we have used "he" throughout the odd-numbered chapters and "she" throughout the even-numbered chapters. The copy is not intended to be sexist.

The Manager's Role as Coach — 2nd Edition

Published by National Press Publications, Inc.
Copyright 2001 National Press Publications, Inc.
A Division of Rockhurst University Continuing Education Center, Inc.

Printed in the United States of America

8 9 10

ISBN #1-55852-256-5

About Rockhurst University Continuing Education Center, Inc.

Rockhurst University Continuing Education Center, Inc. is committed to providing lifelong learning opportunities through the integration of innovative education and training.

National Seminars Group, a division of Rockhurst University Continuing Education Center, Inc., has its finger on the pulse of America's business community. We've trained more than 2 million people in every imaginable occupation to be more productive and advance their careers. Along the way, we've learned a few things — what it takes to be successful … how to build the skills to make it happen … and how to translate learning into results. Millions of people from thousands of companies around the world turn to National Seminars for training solutions.

National Press Publications is our product and publishing division. We offer a complete line of the finest self-study and continuous-learning resources available anywhere. These products present our industry-acclaimed curriculum and training expertise in a concise, action-oriented format you can put to work right away. Packed with real-world strategies and hands-on techniques, these resources are guaranteed to help you meet the career and personal challenges you face every day.

Legend Symbol Guide

Exercises that reinforce your learning experience

Questions that will help you apply the critical points to your situation

Checklists that will help you identify important issues for future application

Key issues to learn and understand for future application

C
A
S
E

S
T
U
D
Y

Real-world case studies that will help you apply the information you've learned

Table of Contents

I NTRODUCTION

"Value the person and enjoy the results."

There are two realities in business today: Get results and keep your result-getters! This is becoming increasingly difficult as globalization, technology and demographic changes bombard today's managers. Add to this the increased roles and responsibilities placed on the manager and chaos erupts.

First, managers were hired to manage — take care of the business. Then, managers had to be leaders — provide vision and mission. Now, they must recruit and train, inspire and motivate, correct and empower. What's a poor manager to do?

The answer is to coach. As a 21st-century manager, you are continually challenged to shift how you, as a leader, manage your most important and only unlimited resource: your people. Henry Kissinger once said, "Leaders take their staff from where they are to where they've never been before." That's what the role of coach lets you do — take a diversely proficient group of people, expand and grow their skills, keep them satisfied and motivated, and, most importantly in this competitive environment, retain their talent.

Reinventing Success

Sports teaches organizations the value of a coach. Whether coaching a team or an individual, different approaches require different skill levels, attitudes and motivation. Business, industry, government and the not-for-profit sectors, likewise, have been faced with the sad truth that people just aren't as motivated and accepting as they were in the last century. Mary Kay Ash noted the change when she said, "There are two things people want more than sex and money ... recognition and praise."

Coaching is the process of using that wisdom to help employees experience and work through the changes required of them.

Societal change caused management to shift from an authoritarian "my way or the highway" style to an all-inclusive approach that requires the manager to be a coach, cheerleader, mentor, trainer, disciplinarian and counselor. Coaches in sports do what organizations must do: create environments where individuals are motivated to produce results. That environment must be supportive, instructive and satisfying to the degree that employees want to grow within it.

The StaffCoaching Model™

The purpose of this book is to give you a model that directs the many roles demanded of your job: getting results, retention and creating a positive environment. Trademarked by National Seminars StaffCoach™ Model, the word "coach" encompasses three distinct roles or approaches: coaching, mentoring and counseling. How you respond to people and choose a specific action depend on your employees' proficiency. Not all your employees need your assistance to change, develop or improve. Often your people can create new behaviors and attitudes themselves. It's a good news/bad news scenario: The good news is that very few people need constant coaching, and the bad news is that all three roles of coaching are needed continuously.

Coaching is an excellent activity for your people who are performing okay. They meet goals and perform tasks at standard — no more, no less. A coach, by definition, helps workers grow and improve their job performance by providing suggestions and encouragement. Mentoring is the best approach for your above-average performers, those who are excelling. The mentor, by definition, is an individual with advanced experience and knowledge who is committed to giving support and career/job advice to a less experienced person. With your people who are performing below average, counseling is the appropriate choice. By definition, counseling is a supportive process to define and correct personal problems or skills that affect performance. The counselor rectifies behaviors and provides direction and discipline as needed for as long as necessary.

This model provides you with a guide to coaching performance. It helps you get around the reality of increasing demand for specialized skills in the workplace and a decreasing talent pool from which to draw. This challenge is captured in the book title by author Jennifer White: The StaffCoach™ Model will allow you to drive your people wild without driving them crazy.

Investing in the Real Resources

Balance sheets and Return on Investment (ROI) statements prove that business typically wastes its greatest resource: the people who work for it. The StaffCoach™ Model teaches you techniques, steps and actions to take as a manager and coach to tap into this asset. Remember the following three critical facts:

1. Management means getting things done through others. Your job, as a leader, is to work through the people who work for you. That's how you'll get results from your team.

    Ferdinand Fournies, who wrote *Coaching for Improved Work Performance*, said, "When you do everything yourself, you're just a technician. When you get things done through others, that's when you become a leader."

    If, as a manager, you are doing any part of your job because "No one else is doing it so I have to" or because "No one does it as well as I do, so I do it," you're probably not getting the best results you could. You're spending time on things that other people ought to do.

2. You need your people more than they need you. Why? Because the only way you're going to get results is through them. You can't do every job. Your time is a limited resource. Only your team can get everything done.

3. You get paid for what your people do ... not for what you do. This is crucial to understand. If it's true that the people who work for you are helping you get results, then you're getting paid for what they're doing.

   In light of these three facts, you can begin developing your skills in coaching, mentoring and counseling. You can best invest your time and energies as a leader in those who produce results. No other investment pays higher dividends than an investment in your people.

It All Comes Down to Winning

Managers who assume the role of coach immediately begin changing attitudes and perspectives, which in turn change behavior and results. Based on the principles used by winning coaches to inspire their teams to excel, *The Manager's Role as Coach* will guide you in making the most of each employee's special talents and harness your group's combined energy to create a results-focused team. The confidence you have in your own abilities and the respect you gain from your staff and management alike will increase. As you use the principles in this manual, you will create an environment where employees enjoy their work, exude positive attitudes, "buy in" to company policies and team goals, and willingly take on added responsibilities.

The benefits of StaffCoaching™ are many. Managers and leaders who can inspire, persuade, influence and motivate can spearhead organizational changes. The model guides you in doing those things necessary to ensure success. The benefits to you personally are equally powerful.

- You increase productivity and get results.
- You increase quality work.
- Your stress level decreases.
- You take less home with you.
- You avoid surprises about poor performance.
- Your job become easier as your people build their skills.
- You can increase your delegation, giving you more personal time.

- You become known as a developer of people.

- You build empowerment through sharing leadership.

- You increase team unity and support, allowing more to get done.

As a coach, you bring an enthusiasm and sense of accomplishment into your workplace. When you are mentoring, you are teaching and developing your people and the organization's future. By counseling, you are eliminating the problems and barriers to real job satisfaction.

Having noted the organization's and your own gains from The StaffCoach™ Model, there remains the *"what's in it for me"* for your people. What's in it for them is simple: excellence, doing their best, reaching their potential. Your coaching means that your people can achieve their goals and take their jobs and careers where they want.

To summarize, The StaffCoach™ Model directly addresses the myriad changes occurring in the workplace today. Diverse demographics, altered needs and increased demands for a fun, enjoyable, self-fulfilling and individualistic work environment can be accommodated to everyone's gain.

Enjoy the manual and your soon-to-increase abilities to persuade, influence, change and grow. Whether your team numbers three or 300, the principles you learn will deliver winning results for you and some of your proudest accomplishments!

CHAPTER 1

Getting Results Is All About You

Value the person and enjoy the results.

Understand Your Role as Coach

"One more job and I quit!" "What do they think I am, a magician?" "I can't juggle any more responsibilities." Sound familiar? Well, get used to it in this frenzied, get-more-done-with-less marketplace. There is a lot more to do and a lot less people to do it; there are a lot more demands from the customers and a lot less ability to fulfill them all; and, there are a lot more questions on how to manage and a lot less answers. There is also a bad news/good news response: The bad news is that you are expected to juggle another role. The good news is that role is to be a coach.

Coaching is not an ability you are born with. Neither does it only relate to sports. It is more than leading a team on the court or the troops in the field. It's more than pumping people up. It is, however, about getting the results that let you sleep at night. It is about how you manage an effective team and a productive group. It's about how you are successful.

Coaching implies motivating, inspiring, taking people to greater heights. It is a directive process by you, a manager, to train and orient an employee to the realities of your workplace, and to assist in removing the barriers to optimum work performance. Coaching is high-level leadership; it's communicating the what, the why and then helping with the how — whether behavioral or attitudinal. You push people and encourage them to push themselves to the highest possible performance. Note the word optimum used earlier to describe the desired result of coaching. There is a difference between optimum and optimal. Optimum is what you want, the best, the most favorable. Optimal is best at that time, given those conditions. You want and must take your people to where they can take the organization: to the greatest levels of productivity.

You take your people to greater levels through understanding your role as a coach. It's more art than science. Just as knowing how to provide good customer service doesn't guarantee that someone will provide that service, so it is with all the management tools you have. Knowing how to create a vision, teaching how to set goals, telling people what their accountabilities are, setting measures, talking career — none of these guarantees optimum performance. The art, the finesse, the skill are found in how you perceive your people, how you dig and probe and discover — no matter how hard and how long — where their strengths are and then get them to buy into that brilliance they possess. Sound like a cheerleader? It's that too! The essence of coaching is getting your people to become what you know they can become. The tools are necessary and valuable, but it's your understanding of coaching that is the impetus for success.

Cultivate the 10 Values of a Successful StaffCoach™

Since coaching isn't something innate, but a skill you can hone and excel in, the StaffCoach™ Model identifies values that great coaches throughout history exhibit. Whether it's Patton or Eisenhower pushing their troops to superhuman feats, Jack Welch or Sam Walton teaching their people how to be the best in their fields, or Arthur Ashe showing his followers how to break out of stereotypes — they share values that underpin their successes. Whatever your role, whatever your field, the following 10 values will guarantee results.

The 10 values of a successful StaffCoach™ include:

1. **Clarity** — giving and receiving accurate communication.

2. **Supportiveness** — a commitment to stand with and behind team members.

3. **Confidence building** — a personal commitment to build and sustain the self-image of each team member.

4. **Mutuality** — a partnership orientation where everyone wins or no one wins.

5. **Perspective** — a total focus on the entire business enterprise.

6. **Risk** — the encouragement of innovation and effort that reduces punishment for mistakes and fosters learning by doing.

7. **Patience** — going beyond the short-term business focus to a view of time and performance that balances long-term gain and business imperatives.

8. **Involvement** — a genuine interest in learning about individuals in order to know what incentives, concerns and actions will inspire them.

9. **Confidentiality** — an ability to protect the information of all team interactions and cause a sense of trust and comfort with the individuals.

10. **Respect** — a giving and receiving of high regard to and from the staff as individuals and members of the team.

Study these values, consider the degree to which you possess them, and make plans to develop them within you.

> *"First say to yourself what you would be; then do what you have to do."*
>
> — Epictetus

Clarity

Successful StaffCoaches™ make sure they communicate clearly. If your communication isn't clear, what happens? People start to fail, do nothing or worse, make assumptions. Huge wastes in money and time often occur because someone *thought* they got it. If you want to make sure your communication is clear, NEVER assume your team members know what you want.

Clarity is the number one tool for success in management. The problem often is that managers think they are clear, that they made sense, but the reality is that they are talking in shorthand. Many managers actually believe they communicate clearly; they hire, assign a task and say, "Go to it, pencils are over there, computer is plugged in, yell if you need anything. Bye." When an associate asks a question, the manager responds, "Sure, that's right" or "You know … ." And you, dear reader, know what likely happens.

> *Assumptions always cost time and money.*

Example

Printer on phone:

Ben, we're ready to print this rush job of yours now, but I thought you said you wanted us to print it in three colors.

Ben/Manager:

I do want three colors.

Printer:

Well, we only got two sets of film from your department. They say that's all you ordered. They gave us film for the red and the yellow.

Ben/Manager:

So, what's missing?

Printer:

It's not all here. Did you tell them to provide black film?

Ben/Manager:

Everyone in the department saw the color layout. Obviously, they knew I would be using black. I certainly wouldn't print photos of people in red or yellow with red and yellow text. That is idiotic!

Printer:

I don't think they understood that or realized that I needed all three sets of film. Whatever! If I have to wait for more film, I can't deliver when you said you needed it …

An understandable oversight? It's easy to forget that black is a color to people who work with film. In this case, however, an understandable assumption cost everyone involved time and money. How can you be sure you're not assuming? Ask questions that reveal what people are thinking. Check for understanding rather than concluding with "Is that clear?"

> *"What have I said that might still be a little unclear?"*

> *"How do you think this approach will work?"*

> *"What kinds of problems do you think we should anticipate?"*

> *"What might you add to this process that would improve it?"*

> *"Tell me what you believe you and I have agreed that you will do."*

Remember, what you "think" you say and what you "actually" say (not to mention what they "think" they hear and what they "actually" hear) are very different things! Clarity isn't exclusively how you communicate to your team members — it's listening and responding to their attempts to open revealing lines of communication.

Example

Coach:

So you and Jim feel good about making this deadline, Mary?

Mary:

We've done it dozens of times.

Coach:

I just want to make sure I can promise the client we'll be there as agreed.

Mary:

Well, you can promise we'll do our part — I can't promise the equipment will hold up under that kind of volume. But we'll find a way. We always do.

Did you hear two messages in that dialogue? The first message was, "We'll do it." The second was, "We might not do it." It's tempting to assume that the first message will prevail, especially when schedules are tight and the client is important or impatient ... or both. It's also easy to not hear the hidden message.

> *"You only succeed when people are communicating, not just from the top down but in complete interchanges. Communication comes from fighting off my ego and listening."*
>
> — Bill Walsh

But an attentive, realistic coach will look into inconsistent messages communicated by his people. If you don't, you risk more than deadline surprise. You risk having your people hear two messages from you: 1) Don't bother me with particulars, just get it done, and 2) Your problems aren't as important to me as how we look to the client.

In this example, the coach may have equipment problems that are about to create client headaches — and may have already created morale problems. Valuing clarity corrects the problem.

Supportiveness

Supportiveness means standing behind the people on your team … providing the help they need, whether that help means advice, information, materials, or just understanding and encouragement. It's important to communicate your intention to be supportive and it's critical that the team knows it.

Let your people know early (individually or in a group setting) that they are part of a unit … a team whose members pull together. Support emphasizes the value of synergy: that 2 + 2 can equal 6 or 8 or 11. Tell the team how you manage: that honest mistakes or problems aren't terminal. Problems will only make the team better as you learn to solve them together. Most importantly, make sure your people know that you are behind them all the way. You exist to help the team win by maximizing individual skills, not by forcing members to do their jobs exactly as you or someone else might. Knowing you will support them, your people can more easily rise to higher levels of performance.

This may have sounded "soft" not too long ago. Many people thought that to be a boss you had to be tough and had to know all the answers, and if you didn't, you had to act like it anyway; if you showed a weakness, you'd lose their respect. Not so today! Those beliefs are no more accurate in a union shop than they are in an administrative office. An example of how you can show responsible support follows.

> *Let your team know that honest mistakes or problems aren't terminal.*

Lead:

This design modification I tried didn't work, Terry. I was sure it would, but they tell me we've got to come up with a new design. That will slow us down at least three days. I guess I blew it.

Coach:

Isn't this the job where you have been trying some different approaches?

Lead:

Yes. We've seen this problem before.

Coach:

Well, naturally, I wish the design had worked — but you're trying things that are new. And this project's been a problem from the start. What if we put two additional people on it? Could we cut a day off the delay time?

Lead:

We probably could.

Coach:

Let's try it. If we make it, we break even timewise. And if we don't, well, you gave it your best shot. Next time, when the time is this tight, let's try brainstorming the design approach with some others before committing to an approach.

Lead:

Good idea. Thanks, Terry.

A different approach, support is midway on a leadership continuum. With control, you call all the shots, and delegating is letting them run it. Managers who control all the time are the ones who don't get the best from their people. If you control the project or plan indiscriminately, people will feel mistrusted and stifled. This is especially true with the Generation X'ers on your staff. Likewise, delegating isn't always teaching by doing. There has to be consideration given to skill level. If they know what they are doing, then let them do it. If they haven't a clue, let them know how to do it. With either, be constant with your support.

Example

Ted (customer service rep on phone):

Hello. This is Ted Stevens.

Customer (on phone):

Mr. Stevens, this is Phil from ACME. We have a problem with the shipment we received this morning from you.

Ted:

Let me get your records up on the computer, Phil. Okay, I've got it. What's the problem?

Customer:

It's incomplete! I spoke with your department head yesterday afternoon and explained how we just had a rush order come in. He promised that he would put an extra 200 shafts on the truck this morning with our regular order.

Ted:

Hmm. I don't see any record here of that. You say Mr. Ingles approved the extra parts to be shipped?

Customer:

I don't know his name, but I told the department head personally that we need them TODAY!

Ted:

Well ... I really don't know what to do for you. My records don't show Mr. Ingles approving the add-on, and I can't ship out more without his signature.

Customer:

Then get Mr. Ingles on the phone for me. We need those parts NOW!

Ted:

Well, uh, Mr. Ingles isn't here right now.

Customer:

Then you take care of it! After all, we've been customers with you for more than 10 years!

Ted:

I'm sorry. I know this is ridiculous, but Mr. Ingles has a strict policy that special orders MUST have his approval, and he won't be in until …

Customer:

Well, you tell Mr. Ingles for me that we won't be bothering you again with orders when they are important to us!

Ted didn't provide very good customer service. He may have been told "the customer comes first," but his boss has made such an issue of "policy" that Ted is afraid, unable or unwilling to break the rules. When managers set down inflexible rules, are they working with their staff or controlling them? When managers control their employees, service can be rendered nil and the customer made to feel totally unimportant. Staff morale also suffers when control erodes support. With retention and recruitment being the number one and number two business challenges today, supportive environments are a real marketplace attractor.

> *When managers control their employees, service often goes down the tubes.*

Confidence Building

Let the people on your team know you believe in them and what they're doing. This is the essence of the coach role: Help people see, feel and intuit their brilliance. Point to past successes … to their individual and team accomplishments. Review with them the actions that caused success and praise the commitment to excellence behind each victory.

One way to do this is to publish a regular list of individual and team accomplishments over the past week or month. Make sure the list is posted in a visible area. Another idea is to have a newsletter distributed to your team members and other key organizational people that summarizes accomplishments. Most importantly, compliment individuals often for jobs well done. One-on-ones are an effective confidence builder. Such actions accomplish three things:

> *Let the people on your team know you believe in them and in what they're doing.*

1. They let team members know you are aware of their efforts to excel.

2. They provide "performance exposure" for members within and beyond the team environment.

3. They encourage people to have a can-do attitude.

Commit to bolstering your people's confidence. Let people know that you know they can do the job and you'll see something wonderful happen: They'll start to get confidence in themselves. They'll start to believe in themselves and accomplish more than even they thought they could.

Mutuality

Mutuality means sharing a vision of common goals. If you as a leader have goals that head one way and your people have goals heading another, the team will fall apart. All too often employees (and sometimes managers) don't have clear-cut goals that everyone understands.

To make sure your team goals are "mutual" — shared by every member — you must take the time to explain your goals in detail. Make sure your team members can answer questions like: Why is this goal good for the team? For the organization? How will it benefit individual members? What steps must be taken to achieve the goal? When? What rewards can we expect when the goal is achieved?

Here's a good example of establishing mutuality in memo form that answers all of those questions. Can you find the answers?

To: Team

From: Marty

Subject: Inventory

As you know, the warehouse is full of new stock we acquired from the recent merger, which has never been inventoried. Our CEO has asked that we conduct an inventory as soon as possible without affecting our production schedule.

So I propose an inventory on the first and third Saturdays of next month from 10 a.m. to 3 p.m. Eight of us should be able to do the entire inventory in that time frame — with time out for company-paid lunches! Attendance isn't mandatory. No pressure. But I would rather not hire temporaries to do this because the funds will have to come out of our miscellaneous account (summer picnic, company nights at the ballpark, etc.).

The suggested inventory schedule allows participants to sleep late on Saturday and leave early enough to have some R&R. Also, volunteers will receive time-and-a-half pay, plus one Friday off between now and Christmas. When this inventory is finished, the CEO estimates that the company could see a 5 percent to 6 percent increase in sales and that our production load for the holidays will be significantly less!

Sign-up sheet is on the bulletin board. To join the fun for one or both Saturdays, you must sign before Friday at 5 p.m.

See you there!

Without goals, mutuality is impossible. You and your team won't go anywhere special. With them, you are destined for greatness!

Perspective

Psychologist George Kelly calls perspective "understanding from the inside out." It's getting inside a person and seeing things from his perspective. Looking at people from the outside in too often results in labeling them. Do you have words and names for people who work for you? Little terms you use to describe them sometimes? Grumpy ... Johnny-come-lately ... The Complainer ... etc.? When we do that, we're understanding people from the outside in instead of the inside out. That means we probably don't understand them at all.

To understand someone from the inside out, you have to ask questions.

> *"What's new in your life, Paul?"*
>
> *"Anything I could do to make it easier for you to complete this project?" (or be at work on time? or feel better about your assignment? etc.)*
>
> *"Why don't we have lunch, Al, and get caught up on how things are going?"*

These kinds of get-involved questions can ultimately reveal who your team members really are. They often disclose medical or family struggles that would make anyone "grumpy" — especially if the boss cares little about employee life beyond the office. These questions reveal the reasons why Johnny comes late and the complainer complains ... reasons for which you might spot obvious and immediate remedies! They allow you to share your perspective with the staff — to grow their outlook so they, also, can see the bigger picture.

For instance, if project delays spring from uncertainties about how to do the job, you might schedule training to provide needed skills and confidence.

If tardiness is the result of having no money to fix an ailing car, you might recommend some creative ways the employee could earn extra dollars, or ask personnel for a list of "carpools" near the employee's home.

If the employee feels resentful about unpleasant job assignments, you might explain in detail the need for the assignment and/or rotate the task between two or more employees.

The more questions you ask, the more you will understand what's going on inside your people. Don't assume that you know what they're thinking and feeling — ask them!

To understand someone from the inside out, you have to ask questions.

Risk

Risk taking is how you grow, learn and excel. The only way you can advance is by taking risks and that is why it is so important to let your people know it's okay to fail — sometimes. Some people who work on your team may do nothing because they're afraid — afraid that if they take a risk and fail you'll be upset. As you learned earlier, to be an effective coach you must communicate that failure is not terminal, as long as everyone learns from it! That's the key. Establish a clear, unthreatening way to deal with errors … a way that starts with the individual. Such a process might have the following five key steps:

1. Outline the specifics of the error with the employees concerned, asking for their help with the details.

2. Identify the cause-and-effect principle involved. (What was the domino that, when pushed, started the process necessary for the error?)

3. Determine at least two ways the same error could always be avoided.

4. Agree on one measurable step (one you can check periodically) that the employees involved will take to avoid making the same error again.

5. Determine logical rewards for correcting the behavior — as well as the exact consequences of continued failure to correct the error.

Example

Employee #1/Bob:

There's no getting around it. We let a typographical error get by in the Annual Report, and all 10,000 are printed already.

Supervisor/Keith:

How did the proofreading phase miss that?

Employee #2/Karen:

Well, because the schedule was so tight, we only spell-checked it through the computer. One of us usually does a final proof, and that didn't happen. So instead of the word

> *The only way you can grow is by taking risks.*

If you never make mistakes, you'll never make discoveries.

"sales," we typed the word "sale." The computer can't tell that's not a correct word.

Supervisor/Keith:

So we skipped a needed project phase to meet the project deadline?

Both:

Yes.

Keith:

How do you think we can avoid this with upcoming projects?

Karen:

I think we need a "check-off" system requiring verification of each phase before the job can move to the next one.

Bob:

That would work. Two of us could do a final proof on critical print projects. Some external projects like the Annual Report might warrant that.

Keith:

Those both sound like great ideas. Karen, could you sketch up what one of those "check-off" forms might look like?

Karen:

Sure.

Keith:

I'll take it with me when I tell Mr. Wells about the mistake. He isn't going to like this, but I think he will appreciate knowing we are taking concrete steps to avoid future errors.

If we can't avoid them, by the way, we might need to hire someone to do nothing but proofread, and there probably wouldn't be enough money in the budget to do that and still have Christmas bonuses.

Successful people have failed, are failing and will fail again. As Tom Peters often says: "Get excited about failures — because only through failures can you learn, grow and be better down the road."

Patience

Most of us hate patience. It's the "P" word. The "P" word goes with the "T" word: time. Yet time is a healer. Every successful StaffCoach™ knows that time and patience are the keys to developing employees and preventing you from simply "reacting" to an issue. Sure, there are times when emergency, on-the-spot decisions must be made.

- When the refrigerated truck carrying your frozen food shipment breaks down somewhere between Fallon and Reno, Nevada

- When a client calls with a great job that's so big it could tax your ability to deliver on time — and if he can't get your answer now, the job will go to someone else

- When the press wants to quote your boss about a citizen complaint and you must either get some facts together pronto for the boss to work from or research the entire complaint for real accuracy — which could take hours

Most managers confirm that such times are surprisingly rare. Even those emergency situations almost always allow you time to ask for a quick word of advice or insight from a respected peer or supervisor.

Generally, however, you can and should avoid knee-jerk responses to unexpected situations. Build some time between the event and your response to it. Use this time to:

1. Evaluate the situation objectively (write it down if possible).

2. Identify alternative solutions with pros and cons for each.

3. Get respected opinions and input.

4. Implement your chosen response.

5. Assess results and alter your approach as needed.

> *"Crisis doesn't make or break you — it reveals you."*
> — Don Moomaw

The best StaffCoaches™ don't react — they act. They use patience to their advantage.

The other equally critical aspect of patience is the ability of the coach to understand that it takes time for people to assimilate change. You have to be patient with people. Some of your team will get it immediately. Others might linger over a step or process to the point that you are grinding your teeth. Patience. Believing in people means believing in the long haul for people to develop. Balance the long-term benefits of developing talent with the short-term business goals whenever you make decisions.

Involvement

Involvement means getting out from behind your desk and going to where your staff is.

Involvement means just that — working with your people. It is caring enough for people to attempt to understand their experiences. It's getting out from behind your desk and going to where your staff is. It's finding out what's going on with your people. It's being interested enough to find out the significant facts about family background, ethnic origins, special hardship situations, ambitions and drive — as well as what types of people they are: shy, outgoing, easy to please, suspicious, etc. It's involving yourself so you can best involve them. Personal knowledge can be the very means by which you convince them to try again, or that it is worth "it."

For example, hearing that one of your foremen will soon be a new father can help explain his recent absentmindedness. But taking extra time to know him better will alert you that the child his wife miscarried several years ago had Down's syndrome. His concerns, therefore, go deeper than mere nervousness and could result in major errors — maybe even an extended absence.

Involving the staff in the management of their own jobs is the other implication of this value. It is a key element in developing employee loyalty and buy in. It helps you know how to motivate team members while allowing them to control their jobs. This is another value that emphasizes the importance of you knowing your people. Different generations react differently. With regard to involvement, for example, the baby boomers, like the Generation X'ers, often as a group are more committed if they are involved.

But it is not essential for them. Past experiences allow them to not be totally turned off if they are not involved. The Generation X cohorts, however, react adversely to being excluded in decisions about their own jobs. Raised largely as latchkey children, many will resist your efforts if you don't collaborate. This stresses the importance of individualizing your approach for each employee while underscoring the universality of the value.

Confidentiality

Confidentiality is the result of the rare ability to keep quiet. Some managers talk when they should be silent — often to prove (usually to themselves) that they are in a position of power. The most successful leaders are those who hold their own counsel. It's the discipline to stop yourself and not give away confidences. The moment you betray a confidence, trust is lost. And when you lose an employee's trust, it's almost impossible to get it back.

This is essential for a coach who deals with people's confidences and their confessions of personal weaknesses and insecurities.

For instance, a manager discovered (through individual performance-appraisal discussions) that two of his employees shared the problem of having alcoholic spouses. Thinking the two might be encouraged by knowing that fact about each other, the manager shared the news with one of them. When the second employee discovered that someone else knew about his problem, he resigned immediately. Moral? Even when sharing confidential information might seem justified, it isn't. Coaching implies privacy.

Once you lose an employee's trust, it's almost impossible to get it back.

Respect

Respect involves a manager's perceived attitude toward the individuals he leads. You may highly esteem your team members, but if they don't perceive that esteem — if it is contradicted by your failure to share goals, your unwillingness to become involved, your inability to exercise patience — you communicate disrespect. Successful coaches show respect by listening, questioning, praising, teaching, providing information. Without respect, the employee is less likely to listen or hear guidance. Knowing he is respected, he will be better able to become involved, share insights and take risks.

Case Study

Chris Early is the creative director for a growing advertising agency. The agency's three top accounts have requested urgent attention to large and unexpected projects — each of which is due about the same time.

After discussing the situation with the agency president, Chris calls a Friday morning meeting with his art directors, his copy chiefs and the account executives for each of the three projects. In that meeting, Chris asks each account executive to explain the project needs and goals and answer any questions that Chris's key people might have. After the meeting, Chris orders in pizza and spends the rest of the afternoon with his leadership team, brainstorming scheduling options, personnel requirements and potential stumbling blocks to meeting the triple deadline.

On Monday morning, Chris calls a meeting of the entire 17-person creative department, in which he announces the upcoming projects. He introduces the three creative directors who will head each project, who in turn outline their project specifics: the teams selected for each as well as the projected timetables.

Chris closes the hourlong meeting by distributing a handout outlining and discussing the goals of each project and the benefits to the agency, as well as announcing the department "awards" picnic that will take place when the projects are completed.

Over the next five weeks of project activity, Chris meets regularly with each project leader and account executive to review progress and any special challenges or difficulties. He attends weekly team meetings, where project leaders and team members on each of the three projects evaluate completed project phases and anticipate possible problems.

When one of the computer illustrators becomes ill, Chris fills in for him until he can return two days later.

As the project deadlines approach, Chris's project leaders recommend hiring two temporary graphics people for one day. Chris agrees. When the three projects are finally completed and approved, one project is completed two days early, one is right on time, and one is a half-day late. None of the other projects in the agency's system during that time fell behind.

Each team member receives a questionnaire asking what he felt went right about each project, what went wrong and how the problems could be avoided next time. Results of the questionnaires are studied and compiled into a full report available to all participants.

Chris invites client representatives to the department picnic for team members and their families. They speak to the group, expressing gratitude and pleasure with project results. Plaques are awarded to each department member for "Most Paranoid" … "Most Oblivious to Pain" … "Most Motivated by Food," etc. And as Chris wraps things up with a few closing remarks, his project leaders dump a cooler of ice water on his head.

Case Study Analysis

1. Listed below are the 10 values of a successful StaffCoach™. Beside each, note how Chris Early exhibited or lacked the value listed.

    Clarity:

    Supportiveness:

    Confidence building:

    Mutuality:

Perspective:

Risk:

Patience:

Involvement:

Confidentiality:

Respect:

2. How do you think members of the department felt about Chris's attitude toward the tasks? Toward them?

3. What do you think was the key to Chris's success? How could that key ingredient help you in the next three months?

4. How would your team members feel about working for someone like Chris? Why?

5. What would you have done differently from Chris? Why?

Case Analysis

Chris's ability to adequately direct the business needs of several top customers while not overwhelming his staff is evident in this case. Many people would jump into the projects without a plan, anticipating overload. The fact that Chris planned before he acted is a contributing factor in the success. Planning early in a project is never wasted; planning early in a project and then effectively communicating to your staff can be taken to the bank (which is one of the strengths of Chris's actions). Although not overly emphasized in this case, there appears to be considerable involvement of Chris's team and appropriate incentives established for hard and effective work. Chris's team knew the workload demand was heavy but there was a company picnic to mark the end. People are much more willing to go above and beyond when they know there is an end in sight. Consider also the benefits of recognizing, rewarding and celebrating results.

One additional comment: Notice the humorous awards presented at the picnic. Although we can only speculate from the case, there appears to be a sense of fun. Like celebration, a fun and enjoyable work environment adds to productivity and morale. That's often an uncommon feature during project crunch time. Any coach who can bring a sense of play into a tense work situation is sensitive to his people's needs. When your team can laugh and have fun along the way, you are setting up high-performance team results.

C
A
S
E

S
T
U
D
Y

What You Value Impacts Your Team

Managers are too often unaware of the impact their values have on other people's lives. The truth is, every day you imprint your values upon your team.

Ask yourself these questions: What kind of values and attitudes do I communicate to the team I lead? Do I signal an attitude of supportiveness, confidence, commitment, mutuality, patience and involvement? Which value or values do I need to add? To eliminate? To answer these questions, try identifying where your attitudes come from. Knowing what you value and why is the key to further developing, changing or adding to the key coaching values.

Have you ever thought about where you got your values? The University of Colorado produced a seminal piece of work on the subject in a video, *What You Are Now Is What You Were Then*, which persuasively demonstrates that your early environment, the people who influence you and the events you experience contribute to who you are today. The people in your life had a significant impact on you because you simply took it all in, with no questioning. Usually those people inspired, taught or corrected you.

In your early years, your parents, teachers and siblings were probably the people who inspired you … challenged you to go further, dream bigger, reach higher. How and what these people taught you are where your values about coaching developed … how they helped you understand the relationship between cause and effect, how they imparted a desire for knowledge, independence, etc. And, of course, they corrected you. Consider the impact on your views about risk taking or patience! In your middle years, usually the people who inspired you were friends … maybe people from your church or public figures or organizations to which you belonged. Your partner may have inspired you … maybe successful athletes … maybe a boss or co-worker. Maybe a drill instructor or aerobic trainer!

When considering the people throughout your life who motivated, taught and corrected you in your many varied endeavors, you probably experienced more correcting and disciplining than praising and being told you can do or be anything you want. That is a common phenomenon in our society, if not

Along the way, someone has made a significant and positive difference in your values.

throughout history, that children get many more don'ts than do's, much more criticism than accolades. What and how you were supported is what has shaped your coaching tendencies.

Anyone reading this book could probably tell a story about a person from the past who made an impact on his life. Along the way, someone made a significant and positive difference in your values. Here is an exercise designed to help you pinpoint those relationships and the values you gained from them. The more knowledge you have, the more capable you are to change behaviors and characteristics.

Exercise: Tracing Your Personal Values History

	1 AGE __ to __			2 AGE __ to __			3 AGE __ to __		
	NAME	POS VALUE	NEG VALUE	NAME	POS VALUE	NEG VALUE	NAME	POS VALUE	NEG VALUE
INSPIRERS									
TEACHERS									
CORRECTORS									

Divide your age into thirds and put those thirds in the three numbered blanks at the top of the chart shown here. For example, if you are 45, write 1–15 in the first blank. In the second blank write 16–30; and in blank three, write 31–45. It doesn't have to be exact. You are dividing your life into three parts.

Now go to the square on the left side that says "Inspirers." To the right of that square, write the names of three people who inspired you in your early years. Move to Column 2 (your middle years) and do the same thing. Then do the same for this part of your life in Column 3.

Next, move to "Teachers" and repeat the process. Think of three people who were your role models, who guided you. Note these for each phase of your life. Last, drop to the bottom of the chart and list three people who corrected you — three people who said "Yes" and "No." Again, consider people in each phase of your life. If you can't think of three names each time, don't worry. As you continue through this manual, other people will come to mind who relate to this exercise. You can return to this page and jot down the name then.

Now in the blocks titled "Positive Value" and "Negative Value," write down the attitudes, ideas or goals that each person you listed communicated to you — the teacher who acted as a coach and especially inspired you, the parent who challenged you to go "above and beyond."

For example, your first column might list "Mom" and "Junior High Principal" as two key figures who provided life inspiration during the first third of your life. Positive inspirational values that mom imparted might include "persistence." Negative values might include "critical of others." The school principal may have inspired you to "aim high," while on the negative side, he may have communicated a tendency toward "perfectionism" ... a feeling that anything less than becoming something like a brain surgeon was not a real job.

Did someone have a major impact on you and help you develop skills that perhaps even you didn't know you had? Remember those people who especially inspired, taught and corrected you, and the attitudes they had that you admired. Are they attitudes you communicate to others daily?

Exercise Analysis

Did you discover some things about yourself? Can you identify where your values and beliefs come from? That's exactly the effect you are having on every one of your team members every day.

Now, based on your past managerial experience and on the values you just identified as being true to yourself, review the 10 values of a successful StaffCoach™ discussed earlier and listed here. Place an "X" after each value in the most appropriate column. Just how do you relate to each value known to be possessed by great coaches?

	I demonstrate these StaffCoach™ values:				
	Always	*Usually*	*Sometimes*	*Rarely*	*Never*
1. **Clarity**					
2. **Supportiveness**					
3. **Confidence building**					
4. **Mutuality**					
5. **Perspective**					
6. **Risk**					
7. **Patience**					
8. **Involvement**					
9. **Confidentiality**					
10. **Respect**					

If you are like the vast majority of managers seeking to improve their leadership skills, this exercise will identify where your strengths are. It will also show you where to focus your attention. Consider the rule of three: Identify the top three areas where you can most benefit and then devote 80 percent of your time developing them.

The checklists, exercises, self-tests, techniques and other tools in this manual are especially assembled to help you see measurable growth in any value area you want to improve. Do all the activities in the book. Return to them in 30 days, review your progress and again assess what to do. Continue with a development plan for yourself and share the tools with your team.

At the beginning of this chapter, you read that great coaches aren't born but are developed. In a real sense, they are "self-made" men and women. Using the tools outlined in this book will help you make yourself, too!

Five Insights of High-Performance Coaches

No coach has ever had the "perfect team." The best teams you've ever seen — the ones you may have wished you had — all have their share of personality types that could drive anyone crazy. The difference between the success and failure of any team is how well the coach understands and motivates team members. Those same aspects that drive people crazy can drive productivity through the roof as well.

To make that happen, a coach must possess five high-performance insights.

1. People behave based on their thoughts.

2. Individuality should be valued and explored.

3. Lack of motivation often reflects discouragement.

4. Consequences determine performance.

5. People treated responsibly take responsibility.

Like being aware of what influenced your values, understanding these insights gives you fuel for change.

> *No coach has ever had the "perfect team."*

People Behave Based on Their Thoughts

If you have an employee who is negative and pessimistic … grumbling and complaining all the time … you can predict exactly how he views life. Negatively. If an employee is generally happy and sees problems as challenges, you can pretty well count on that person to have a positive outlook on life.

As a coach, you need to understand the "philosophies" of the people who work for you.

Some of those philosophies, conscious and unconscious, include the following:

- Work is what I do to fund my weekends.

- If life gives you lemons, make lemonade.

- This job is a rung on my ladder to success.

- No one can do everything, but everyone can do something.

- Humor: Don't leave home without it.

- Whatever's wrong, I didn't do it.

- Know your limits, then break through them.

- If you learn from losing, you're a winner.

Recognize anyone you know? In some cases, you may need to help team members rewrite those philosophies. How? If a very negative or uncommunicative person works for you, your natural reaction is to avoid that person. But as a coach, you'll never understand what makes that employee tick unless you spend time with him. You have to get close enough to understand the person's attitude or action.

For instance, negative people sometimes develop outward attitudes to mask inner feelings of inferiority. Make sure they believe you feel they are capable, valuable team members.

Coach:

You know, Jeff, I've been thinking about what you said about that last project being a waste of time, and I think you may have had a point.

Some minds are like concrete — all mixed up and permanently set!

28

Jeff:

About what?

Coach:

We do waste a lot of time around here sometimes. I think the newer people would really benefit from your experience identifying those time-wasters.

Jeff:

What do you mean?

Coach:

I was hoping you would consider doing a short presentation on how to plan effectively for a project. After all, no one knows how to plan better than you do.

Helping an employee develop a positive perspective is essential, but be honest in your methods. Don't make up affirming things to say about an employee. But don't be afraid to challenge the employee's attitudes with additional job involvement. The result can mean new levels of productivity.

Individuality Should Be Valued and Explored

Too many leaders don't allow their people to be unique and creative. Instead, they distrust individuality and smother the people on their team. They see disagreement or argument as bad. They inadvertently cultivate a team of clones — people who respond to every situation just as they would. That's not coaching — and it's not how you get the best out of your team.

Each of the people on your team has unique capabilities and creative resources. If you have five team members, then you have five creative resources besides your own. How do you know what those unique gifts are? Assuming your team is fairly new, you could ask the people whom your team members have previously worked for. You could review team members' original resumes, job applications and/or performance reviews. Or you could just ask them!

One way to ask them directly is through an informal questionnaire. While you will want to tailor this tool to your specific needs, a generic "Talent Inventory" might include questions like the following:

- What are your special job strengths as a member of our team?

- What would you say your weaker areas might be?

- If you were tackling a project to (name a project relative to your environment), what responsibilities would you enjoy most? Which would you feel most qualified for? Least qualified for?

- If your team could know only one thing about you, what should that one thing be?

- If you could expand your knowledge and skill level in any area of our duties as a team, what area would you like that to be?

Working together will naturally reveal more about the talents and potentials of your entire team, but little tools like the above questionnaire can greatly help. You may discover that Jane can supervise projects and Joe has a knack for details. When you start tapping the creativity and uniqueness of the people on your team, you create a dynamic called "synergy." The creativity of each member contributes to the creativity of the group, becoming something greater than what you or any one individual could accomplish. This is another example of the value of diversity on a team. As a coach, you can capitalize on diversity to have a high-performing team where members learn from one another.

It is helpful in grasping this concept to think of the words "symphony" and "energy" coming together in one word — "synergy." It's as if you are a conductor, coaxing the individual notes (energy) from each person who contributes to the whole (symphony). Don't be a boss who thinks that everyone has to conform, who is threatened by or distrustful of the creativity of the group.

Team members who excel in the organizational aspects of a task should ideally be involved in planning, scheduling, tracking, etc. Team members whose talents are primarily creative might be involved in concept development and product refinement. Even when such specialization isn't possible ... when the job

Let your people express their individuality within the project framework.

description does not fully reflect an employee's primary aptitude … be open to modifications that can benefit the team! For instance, a person whose responsibilities are basically clerical might exercise creative talent by developing a team logo or banner as time permits. The point is, let your people express their individuality within the project framework. Not only will you see tremendous gains in productivity, but staff morale will increase dramatically as well.

Lack of Motivation Often Reflects Discouragement

When people are not motivated, it's often because they are discouraged, not because they are lazy, stupid or ill. Find out why they're discouraged. If you can identify that … and then be creative in your encouragement … the missing motivation can suddenly begin to surface.

How do you find out the reason for the discouragement? For starters, try the same source that told you about the problem in the first place. If the source isn't the individual in question, you must verify it with the team member personally. However, discouragement can show itself in many other ways: a decrease in productivity, less attention to detail, tardiness, absenteeism, etc.

Ultimately, a one-on-one "RAP" meeting is a good way to confront the problem. RAP is a coaching acronym that stands for:

Review the past.

Analyze the present.

Plan the future.

With this approach, you and the team member can focus on a review of past performance contrasted with present performance — and then look together to an improved future. This simple tool is logical and easy to remember. When the RAP approach is followed, most coaches have no difficulty keeping track of where the meeting is going and what progress has already been made.

Another plus of the RAP model is its emphasis on future solutions. Discussions of the past and present are much less important than planning for the future, especially since the goal is to help team members work closer to their potential.

R

A

P

31

Example

Coach:

Jenny, I really like the way your company newsletter has caught on and the way you are handling it along with all your other duties.

Jenny:

I enjoy it.

Coach:

I can tell! I don't know if you realize it or not, but you have averaged working about three more hours per week since you began doing this newsletter, and you haven't been late to work once in the last four weeks.

Jenny:

I knew I was probably working a little harder.

Coach:

You really are. I think you have solved the attendance problem we talked about last February. The newsletter idea was a great way to make use of your interests!

Remember, the "P" in RAP makes the process work. Help your team members identify goals that excite them and maximize their capabilities.

Consequences Determine Performance

The best way to change performance is to carry out appropriate consequences. Consequences are essential! If an employee constantly performs unsatisfactorily, examine the consequences of that behavior. If no negative consequences exist, guess what? The behavior will continue. And if no positive consequences exist for changing the behavior, guess what? No change. The consequences (negative or positive) must fit the behavior in order to change it — and they must be implemented immediately and consistently.

The best way to change performance is to carry out appropriate consequences.

Example

A group of businessmen in Olathe, Kansas, decided that they needed to lose weight. So they started a contest — the winner to be honored by the losers. However, half the men, recalling their past records of failure, decided to approach the weight loss a little differently. They elected to record each member's weight weekly. Any participant who did not lose at least one pound each week paid $10 to every member who had lost one pound. Which group do you suppose lost weight faster? You guessed it. When it comes to measurable change, consequences are king!

People Treated Responsibly Take Responsibility

Team members who are viewed as responsible for their actions tend to take responsibility. Have you noticed that when someone gives you responsibility, you tend to rise to that level of trust? The same thing happens with the people on your team. As you give them responsibility, they will rise to it. And when you do that, you also help that team member develop pride, self-respect and loyalty!

If a member of your team performs unsatisfactorily, take a few minutes to review the five insights of high-performance coaches. Usually, the key to the person's bad behavior and the remedy to the problem lie in one of these five key insights!

Case Study

Jennifer and Paul recently assumed StaffCoaching™ roles in the same division of a large greeting-card firm. Both were supervisors before their promotions. Both wrote down their plans as new StaffCoaches™ for their respective departments.

Jennifer said she looked forward to defining the auditing department challenges her team faced and then providing the team with well-defined goals and standards. Because of her job knowledge, she also planned to prepare a detailed performance model for each employee. She felt this approach would assure consistency in goals and performance standards and measure job and performance progress.

Paul said he had enrolled in a management-skills seminar to make sure he understood the coaching process. In the meantime, he planned to involve his accounts receivable group in day-to-day planning, organizing and problem solving. He felt his job experience was a strong plus but wanted every member of his team to contribute to the group's effectiveness. Paul also said team members need the growth that comes from being involved in a project.

Which of these StaffCoaches™ would you like to work for? Why?

Analysis

Jennifer and Paul both recognize the importance of goals and plans. Employees who have limited knowledge or experience may appreciate Jennifer's approach because they have more to learn. Her standards and models will provide needed guidance. As they learn under her coaching style, however, they may soon feel reluctant to share their own job ideas. New work methods plus simpler and better ways to achieve objectives might be rare under Jennifer's leadership. Experienced employees may feel an immediate sense of confinement.

Experienced employees will appreciate Paul's approach because it provides a needed outlet for involvement. They will feel free to help the team effectiveness while working on their own.

Employees with lesser skills will feel encouraged to learn so they too can become more productive and contribute. Paul's team will respect his decision to participate in StaffCoach™ training, seeing it as a willingness to commit to and invest in each team member.

Summary

As a manager, your main role is to coach your people. Developing the most valuable assets of your organization requires skills that are learned, and that are more art than science. The approaches you take as a coach — inspiring, teaching, correcting — are based on your assessment of your people's performance. How effective you are is influenced by your values. There are 10 values that effective coaches have. Learn where you are in terms of each value. Assess the origin of your beliefs and values. Determine how you feel about the five insights that effective coaches share.

Aligning your own beliefs, thoughts and values to those of successful coaches gives you the impetus for change. Change yourself and you can change your team.

Chapter Quiz

1. What does "management" mean?

2. Why are people "unlimited resources"?

3. Name the 10 values of a successful StaffCoach™.

4. What does the acronym RAP mean?

5. List as many ways as you can to better understand the unique talents and abilities of each team member.

The Five-Step StaffCoaching™ Model

*Give people permission and confidence
to do their job.*

Coaching Is a Performance Process

How do the great managers — the Tommy Lasordas, the Barbara Jordans — inspire and develop their people? One word: process. They don't coach or counsel, mentor or teach and say, "Okay, now that's done." They see coaching as a performance process, with lots of steps and actions, that goes on continually. Their leadership values and insights impact everything they do, influence how they spend their time, and where and with whom they devote their energy.

The StaffCoach™ Model shapes the process for you, by guiding your decisions on who, when and how to coach your team and manage your tasks more meaningfully. It uses accomplishments as a source of motivation for people. Thomas Edison's response, when asked how great it must be to be inspired and then invent something, illustrates this. He replied, "No, I invent something and then I get inspired." StaffCoaching™ gets the results that inspire your people. The results you want come from constant movement, not accepting and not staying with the average.

To begin this process, understand a basic but universal truth: No matter where you are, no matter how many people you put together on a team, you will always experience the same phenomenon. Some team members will perform above expectations ... some will perform at an average or standard level ... and some will perform at substandard levels.

This is true regardless of training, experience or similar background. In *Coaching for Improved Performance*, Ferdinand Fournies pointed out that people performed differently and had different needs, and it was pointless to ask them what they needed or where they were at any given time. He said few people could accurately assess how they did and even fewer could articulate it if they did know. As a successful StaffCoach™, you have to know where people are on any given task and how they're doing overall. You must deal with each of these performance levels differently — that's what the Five-Step StaffCoaching™ Model is all about. The Five-Step StaffCoaching™ Model is a highly effective framework that provides managers with proven techniques for achieving greater results from their people. It recognizes that people are dynamic. They approach different situations and different days with varying performance levels.

To implement this simple but powerful model, the first thing you must assess is the current performance level of each team member. What are the standards for each person's performance? Is the person you're evaluating performing above the standard, working at the standard level or performing below standard? It is important here to remember the value of perspective. You have the overall performance of the person, and you must also distinguish the different skills, aptitudes and competencies per her different responsibilities.

One helpful way to arrive at answers to these essential, beginning questions is to compile information about each team member on a form like the one shown here. It doesn't have to be a complicated form and can easily be digitized. It isn't intended to function as a formal performance-evaluation report — only as a worksheet for establishing initial leadership direction.

A good tip is to keep a file of your approaches, different options and your people's preferences and strengths. Constantly reassess, plan and adapt.

Performance Assessment

Name _____

Basic Responsibilities	Obvious Strengths	Obvious Weaknesses	Overall Assessment of Performance Historically (Superior, Average, Substandard)	Performance During Last Year	Immediate StaffCoach™ Action

2

Once you have clearly identified where each team member is in her individual development and how that performance impacts the team, you will be ready to move on with specific steps that maximize each team member's growth potential. Remember, the performance level and the individual guide you in choosing a StaffCoach™ role.

> *The way to get anywhere is to start from where you are.*

Steps in the StaffCoach™ Model to Maximize Potential

Step No. 1. "Assess Present Performance," is where success starts, as illustrated on the Five-Step StaffCoaching™ Model shown here. Once you have established your employee's present performance level, you are ready to 2) coach, 3) mentor or 4) counsel, as the situation warrants. This is why different behaviors are required for different people and different behaviors may be required for the same person. How you coach depends on your assessment of the situation, the requirements and the results. This explains why even though predictable bosses are appreciated and enjoyed, they aren't always effective. Teaching the old leadership styles of autocrat, democrat or free rein fall short regardless of personality or need because of the reality of diversity within an individual and within a team. You may use only one approach with an individual and you may use two or all three with the same person. It depends on her performance.

StaffCoaching™: The Coaching Process

Step No. 2. If a person is achieving average or standard performance, you'll respond in the role of coach.

Step No. 3. For those delivering above-average performance, you respond in the role of mentor.

Step No. 4. Team members operating at below standard performance need your involvement in the role of counselor.

2

Step No. 5 is the ongoing act of integrating each team member … at whatever performance stage she exhibits … into the team in a positive, productive and fulfilling role. This team result can be understood as collaboration, with your employees working individually and as a group to optimize each other's performance.

Begin with assessment — what is happening now. Don't let your thoughts ever waver from the results you want as you assess. Think of this as a backward process: This is what excellent performance looks like, this is what we need, this is how she is performing. So, what do I do? Trainers discuss this as identifying the gap between what the person is doing and what the person ideally could be doing. With the result clear in your mind, you focus the choices. Always ask, "So what?" and "Who cares?" — "so what" brings you to what you currently have and "who cares" keeps you tracking results. Start with the employee and end with you: What is she doing and what do I need to do? In Total Quality Management (TQM) literature, there is a saying about the American versus the Japanese approach to planning. The difference is explained by noting that the Americans have a very fast trigger and a slow bullet while the Japanese have a slow trigger but a very fast bullet. This adage often explained why the Japanese, slower to action, generally had error-free results.

Know Your Employees' Character and Capabilities: Four Effective Techniques

Personal Observation

StaffCoaching™ requires firsthand knowledge of, and one-on-one familiarity with, your team members and their jobs. There is no way around that; the value of involvement does pay off here. Knowing where your people are and why gives you an ability to connect your coaching. The better you know your people, the better you can target your coaching to what is important to them. Knowledge gives you more than rapport; it lets you click with the others.

41

2

The better you know your people, the better you can make the right game-winning decisions.

Not surprisingly, therefore, assessing the performance levels of your team members starts with developing firsthand information about each person on the team.

To cover all the bases, let's assume you are totally new to your team. You have just signed on and are ready to meet and evaluate team members. Let's further assume that you are already familiar with the overall team function and individual job descriptions that contribute to team success. How do you become familiar with each team member and how well she is doing the job at hand?

Undoubtedly you will have talked with your supervisors (if any) about job personnel and job challenges as they perceive them. But the task of evaluating an employee's performance does not start with other people. It starts with the team member. Why? Because your own firsthand impressions and opinions are key to performance objectivity. The time will come when the thoughts of others can and should be weighed, but not before you have firsthand impressions of the personalities, problems and potentials that create your unique team mix.

The Face-to-Face Phase

Talk to your employee. Find a time when you are both free to spend at least 30 minutes to an hour in uninterrupted, casual conversation, and schedule a comfortable "get to know each other" chat. The goals of your time together will be threefold.

If you are a manager, even of insignificant things, you'll never be an insignificant manager.

Understand:

1. What motivates your employee.

2. What problems and pluses (professional and personal) she perceives about performing daily tasks.

3. What goals she has for career growth and development.

While insights into each of these areas could surface during random, undirected conversation, many managers find that asking nine specific questions usually achieves the above three goals. Naturally, you will want to modify these questions to better suit your own situation, but the nine questions are as follows:

1. What do you like best about your job?

2. What do you like least?

3. What has satisfied you most about your job performance in recent months?

4. What has frustrated you most about project duties?

5. What is the thing you feel you contribute best as a member of our team?

6. What changes have you recommended in your job over the past year?

7. What training has best prepared you to do what you do?

8. Are there aspects of your job for which you feel unequipped in any way?

9. What is the one area of your job you would like to improve in?

These questions give you insights that guarantee your coaching will connect. You will want to phrase these nine questions in a way that feels comfortable to you. But when workers are questioned during the employee/coach "face-to-face phase," employees will usually give you the information you need to proceed to the next phase.

Caution: Rather than ask these questions from a list or make notes during your employee's responses, let the questions sound spontaneous and conversational. While it is natural that, as a coach, you inquire about the person, it isn't helpful to sound like you are grading the team member. Immediately after the discussion, you can record your question-by-question impressions and recollections, but not while you are talking.

The Recap Phase

In addition to recording concrete responses to the nine questions posed, it is also helpful to record your impressions of the discussion on a form that focuses on some of the more intuitive, subjective or abstract aspects of the meeting. Why? Because you are attempting to determine the correct StaffCoach™ approach needed by each team member: coaching, mentoring or counseling. All the data you can gather to help your employee in this regard should be considered. Toward that end, many coaches have found the following post-interview form to be a valuable tool for

> *"Coaching is hard to explain. I'm not a psychologist — I think it all comes down to a disciplined will."*
> — Vince Lombardi

assessing team member development needs. Remember that while this example presumes your staff is new to you, it is a dynamic process. As situations change, new people or tasks come along, accountabilities shift and results are demonstrated, you must reassess your approach. One change potentially affects everything.

Recap Form

_____   _____
Team Member Name   **Date**

	Not Evident								Very Evident
Commitment to job/ organization	1	2	3	4	5	6	7	8	9	10
People tolerance	1	2	3	4	5	6	7	8	9	10
Project tolerance	1	2	3	4	5	6	7	8	9	10
Self-starter	1	2	3	4	5	6	7	8	9	10
Desire to excel	1	2	3	4	5	6	7	8	9	10
Willingness to learn	1	2	3	4	5	6	7	8	9	10
Responsive to constructive criticism	1	2	3	4	5	6	7	8	9	10
Openness to new job direction	1	2	3	4	5	6	7	8	9	10
Self-confidence/esteem	1	2	3	4	5	6	7	8	9	10

Total _____

Add the numbers in each column and total them. A score of 27 or less probably indicates a need for counseling and/or coaching in several areas. A score of 54 or less points to the likelihood of coaching in several performance areas. A score of 63 or better indicates that greater results would come from mentoring.

This form can be useful for you in interview situations when you are evaluating skills and aptitude. The questions elicit insights that give you an edge on determining who can do what and how.

On-the-Job Contact

No understanding of employee aptitude and performance is complete without observing the employee in the actual job setting. This will be easier in some environments than others, of course. Evaluating an assembly line technician is easier than evaluating a writer. Or observing a CAD operator is easier than assessing a computer programmer. Nonetheless, your collective impressions from viewing each team member on the job will contribute to your overall assessment of that person's attitudes and aptitudes.

What exactly are you looking for? Although the following checklist is very general, it should provide basic working guidelines for observing and evaluating members of your team. Note how the elements positively guide results, regardless of the job or industry. It is as useful for your front-desk professional as it is for your line personnel or the independent contractor.

Add the numbers in each column and total them. A score of 27 or less probably indicates a need for counseling and/or coaching in several areas. A score of 54 or less points to the likelihood of coaching in several performance areas. A score of 63 or better indicates a primary need for mentoring.

On-the-Job Evaluation Form

Team Member Name   **Date**

	Not Evident									Very Evident
On-the-job confidence	1	2	3	4	5	6	7	8	9	10
Tolerance for stress	1	2	3	4	5	6	7	8	9	10
Standards of excellence	1	2	3	4	5	6	7	8	9	10
Attention to detail	1	2	3	4	5	6	7	8	9	10
Innovation	1	2	3	4	5	6	7	8	9	10
Flexibility/openness to alternatives	1	2	3	4	5	6	7	8	9	10
Ability to teach, model	1	2	3	4	5	6	7	8	9	10
Acceptance by peers/superiors	1	2	3	4	5	6	7	8	9	10
Speed	1	2	3	4	5	6	7	8	9	10

Total _____

Supervisory/Personnel Information

Again assuming, as we are, that you are new to this team environment, the ability to obtain the evaluations and assessments of supervisors and/or personnel files will be very helpful in determining the performance level of your team members.

What are you looking for?

- **Performance reviews**

  Any insights and information you can gain from the recorded evaluations of previous managers will be helpful in gauging team member strengths, problems or potential.

- **Supervisor insights**

  If your team is large enough to include supervisory personnel, then you should carefully evaluate their views and performance appraisals of team members' attitudes, aptitudes and actions at this point. (Obviously, your evaluation of the supervisors themselves would affect this data.)

- **Coaching approach used in the past**

  This allows you to assess if what was done in the past with this employee or the team was effective and should be repeated. General Patton's retort, when told to retreat, that he never bought the same real estate twice is apropos here. Why repeat what had little effect?

One way to standardize supervisory input to the performance-evaluation process is to employ a five-point form like the one on the following page. Each supervisor should be asked to complete one of these forms for each of the team members.

> *"The price of greatness is responsibility."*
> — Winston Churchill

Supervisory Observation Form

1. My overall impression of this employee's skill level relative to her job description is

2. I believe this individual excels in

3. This person can benefit from

4. My assessment of this person's professional improvement over the last one to two years is

5. My recommendation for this employee in the immediate future is

2

Extra Departmental Observations

If your team interacts regularly with other people, departments or divisions, the observations of selected professionals can often enlighten you about the perceived performance of your team members. This is one benefit of the 360-degree performance appraisal. Remember: The key word here is "perceived." The opinions of those who interact only occasionally with your people should be considered only as they support the overall weight of departmental opinion.

Caution: This method can be the least trustworthy way to assess a team member's performance level. Depending on your special situation, however, it can add some weight to your employee's performance appraisal. Likewise, seeking insight from team members is dangerous. The value of confidentiality is diminished.

Input From the Individual

Finally, seek input from the individual in order to understand her professional motivation, problems and career goals. While you have already conferred one-on-one with each team member, allowing each person to respond to a short informal questionnaire gives the employee the chance to expand on ideas she may have only touched on in your face-to-face discussion. One such questionnaire ("Talent Inventory") was suggested in Chapter 1 (page 30). Here is another questionnaire on the next page.

Individual Questionnaire

1. One of the ways I have felt most challenged in my job is

2. One aspect of my job I have felt least inclined to perform is

3. If given the chance, I believe I can exceed my job requirements by

4. One of the ongoing frustrations of my job is

5. My professional goal is to

Review Insights: Combine and Consider

Review and analyze the various insights. Look for patterns and note any discrepancies. Study the evaluation tools and again compare and combine the different perceptions.

- Recap Form
- On-the-Job Evaluation Form
- Supervisory Observation Form
- Individual Questionnaire

Completing the entire performance-evaluation process gives you a good idea where each employee falls in the overall team picture. Obviously, your assessment isn't definitive but indicates where and how you can begin to support performance. Your evaluation of individual team members will change regularly as additional job performances are observed. Until then, your initial performance evaluation is a necessary step to encourage each employee to produce at an optimum level.

As stated earlier, some employees will be performing above expectations … some at average or standard levels … some at substandard levels. Some will be excellent at certain aspects of their jobs and substandard in other aspects. The process is dynamic.

The difficulty in analyzing and evaluating performance is that, as a manager, you probably have dealt with the "entire job" and haven't assessed specific accountabilities and isolated performances per se. By clarifying in measurable terms how each employee is a mix of performance levels, each possibly requiring a different StaffCoaching™ approach — coaching, mentoring, counseling — you can have a huge impact on the employee's growth.

Before determining the what and how of each StaffCoach™ approach, consider your own strengths and preferences. Add some self-insight and you can better guarantee that what you do is based on what is appropriate and less the result of habit or comfort. What is your strongest approach — coaching? mentoring? counseling? The StaffCoaching™ Style Inventory will help you recognize where your strengths lie.

> *"Greatness lies not in being strong, but in the right use of strength."*
> — Henry Ward Beecher

> *"Every great work is at first impossible."*
> — Thomas Carlyle

51

Your StaffCoaching™ Style

StaffCoaching™ Style Inventory

Supervisors and managers find themselves in critical incidents that require on-the-spot decisions. This inventory will help you identify your "StaffCoaching™ Style."

Rank your response to each situation, giving three (3) points for your top choice, two (2) for your second preference and one (1) for your least-desired choice in each scenario.

1. Two employees in your department do not get along. One of them has asked you to intervene. You say …
    - _____ a. "Why should I get involved? You work it out, or come to me together."
    - _____ b. "I'll talk to the other party," thinking you'll get to the bottom of this before it gets out of hand.
    - _____ c. "Can you give me some background? Maybe we can work this out together."

2. During a staff meeting, one employee charges that your leadership efforts are a joke, that nothing gets done. After the meeting, you say …
    - _____ a. "Let's discuss this privately."
    - _____ b. "Let me state the goals of this project again."
    - _____ c. "I'm really concerned about your response. What do you mean?"

3. During a private conversation with another supervisor, you find out that her job may be eliminated. You say …
    - _____ a. "Let's explore the available options, okay?"
    - _____ b. Nothing, but probe to gain more information.
    - _____ c. "Do you want to talk about it?"

4. Personnel cuts must be made in your department. A meeting has been planned to announce the cuts, but another manager has cold feet and may not show up for the meeting. You say …
    - _____ a. "I understand your concern about giving bad news, but we're expected in this meeting. Let's look at some ways we can do this together."
    - _____ b. "You've got to be there. Think of the long-term reactions if you're not."
    - _____ c. "What do you think we can do so it's easier on both of us?"

5. You are assigning work responsibilities and identify a major conflict in the work priorities of an employee on your team. You say …
    - _____ a. "I really respect your thoughts and feelings on this. Let's talk about priorities."
    - _____ b. "I've got the jobs pretty well assigned and can't switch now. You've got to change what you're doing."
    - _____ c. "There's a logical way to meet both our goals. Let's see if we can find mutual priorities."

6. Your manager has called you to her office and asked your opinion about an employee who is not in your department. You say …
    - _____ a. "Can we talk about the goals and objectives before I give any opinions?"
    - _____ b. "You're talking to the wrong person."
    - _____ c. "I'm really glad you are checking out our employees. Let me tell you what I think."

7. A major deadline is about to expire on one of your best accounts. You need every resource to meet the deadline, but one employee is very upset over family problems. You say …
    - _____ a. "This project must get out the door. What can you do?"
    - _____ b. "The show must go on; you'll have to leave personal business at home."
    - _____ c. "One option is to call the client and see if we can get an extension for your part."

StaffCoaching™ Style Inventory (Continued)

8. Every person in your unit has complained about the work of one person. In a team meeting, you have asked for work-specific feedback that could help the team, but no one speaks up. You say …
   - _____ a. "We must get past the problems, so I'll start, but I expect the rest of you to join in."
   - _____ b. "This is unacceptable! I know there are problems. Who's going to speak up?"
   - _____ c. Lightheartedly, "I guess there are no problems that you can't handle individually. I'll move on if no one has anything to add."

9. Over the past few weeks, it seems that employees have consistently ganged up on one worker. Every staff meeting is attack time. You say to the employee …
   - _____ a. "I think you need to develop a strategy for getting through those attacks."
   - _____ b. "Why don't you speak up? What do you need right now?"
   - _____ c. "You don't have to be the target, unless you want to. You must really feel under attack. Let's find some way to stop the attacks."

10. Projects are way behind and during a problem-solving session, one member begins to cry. You say …
    - _____ a. "Let's take a break," thinking you can work with the person and allow time to recover.
    - _____ b. "I understand that you're upset."
    - _____ c. "Let's look at this and see how to get out of this mess."

Scoring: Add up the columns. Now, starting on the left side, write the word "Coach" in the far left box. In the middle box, write the word "Mentor," and in the box at the right, write the word "Counselor." Your highest score will tell you what your primary strength is likely to be. You should also look at your lowest score — that's where you are probably weak.

1.	c. _____	a. _____	b. _____
2.	b. _____	c. _____	a. _____
3.	b. _____	a. _____	c. _____
4.	a. _____	c. _____	b. _____
5.	c. _____	a. _____	b. _____
6.	a. _____	c. _____	b. _____
7.	a. _____	c. _____	b. _____
8.	b. _____	c. _____	a. _____
9.	b. _____	a. _____	c. _____
10.	b. _____	c. _____	a. _____

TOTAL _____   TOTAL _____   TOTAL _____

Analysis of Your Preferences and Tendencies

Your highest score tells you what your primary strength is likely to be. Look at your lowest score. Depending on how big the gap, this could indicate a weakness or a possible avoidance of this activity. Consider just how accurate these scores are.

What difference does it make whether or not you prefer a certain style or avoid another? Again, it is a matter of habit, comfort and avoidance. You can become comfortable switching among approaches depending upon several factors: First, how much you have used each approach in the past, or had it used for you; second, how well you used an approach and how it fit in your overall perception of just what your role was. You may be more effective or less effective interacting with your people in a particular style. But knowing your stylistic tendencies as a StaffCoach™ can help you:

1. Overcome natural inclinations to use a style you prefer but that may not meet an employee's immediate needs.

2. Understand which StaffCoach™ style will require additional effort and study on your part (to be discussed) if you are going to provide balanced leadership.

Most managers are strongest in counseling skills. Think about it. What do people usually think is the job of the manager? If you hesitate, consider what first pops into people's minds when they get a note from you saying "see me." Supervision usually correlates with correction and discipline. Most managers are weakest in mentoring for several reasons.

1. The majority of people have never experienced mentoring so it's a hard approach to model.

2. Much mentoring is, in fact, one-sided: the employee waiting for direction and the mentor wondering "why me?" In the past, in fact, many people resented mentoring, feeling it was a drain on time.

3. Mentoring takes two things: the "P" word and the "T" word. Patience and time — two commodities that managers (and professionals in general) find increasingly difficult to spare.

4. Mentors get close and they care. Those can be scary emotions.

Six Pitfalls to Your StaffCoaching™ Success

Adopting an ineffective style negatively affects results. There are other pitfalls, as well.

Let's pretend for a moment. Pretend that instead of wanting to be a motivational coach who inspires others to do their best, you want to undermine the team. You want the team to fail. Ridiculous? Unfortunately, it happens every day. It's not that managers consciously want their teams to fail. It's just that without thinking, they do things that would defeat any team. Often this is a natural occurrence because of the way they were managed. This is a continual caution for you: Think about how and why you act as you do with your staff. Avoid doing things because that's just the way it is.

The following six actions are practically guaranteed to demoralize your people and keep them from reaching their goals. BEWARE OF THESE PITFALLS!

1. Talk at your employees, not with them.
2. Exaggerate situations or behavior.
3. Talk about attitudes rather than behavior.
4. Assume the employee knows the problem and solution.
5. Never follow up.
6. Don't reward improved behavior.

Managers should talk with team members — not at them.

Talk at Your Employees, Not With Them

This killing tendency is all too common. When you talk at someone, you're talking down to her. You're being condescending. Often this kind of approach is accompanied by pointing a finger or pen, and the frequent use of words like "I want" and "you should." It can't even be called "giving orders" — it is attacking people with rank and the threat of retribution. The result? Over time, team

2

members will either leave or, perhaps worse, gradually become what your tyrannical style is teaching them to be: responsive only to direct orders ... not self-starters ... distrustful of management ... uncommitted to your vision ... unmotivated to operate beyond performance minimums. This absolutely destroys any connection or rapport with the person you are trying to reach.

Managers should talk with team members. One of the best ways to do this is to start using the words "we," "our" and "us."

> *"We've got our work cut out for us in order to make the deadline we committed to."*
>
> *"Well, we blew it on that order. Let's figure out what we learned and do our best not to repeat the error."*

Exaggerate Situations or Behavior

You are guaranteed to drag people down when you correct behavior using words like "always," "never," "all the time" and "everybody." Generalizations attack the self-esteem of the individual. If you tell someone, "You're always late" or "You never do this" or "Everyone feels this way," you aren't telling the truth! No one is "always" anything. The moment you use "absolute" words, your employee feels attacked. Instead of generalizations, be specific — and remember that your role of authority calls for insight ... not insensitivity! This is definitely a turnoff.

Talk About Attitudes Rather Than Behavior

When you criticize attitudes rather than behavior, you're setting up failure. Consider something like this in a performance review: "You do this real well, and I appreciate what you're doing here, but the problem I see is your attitude."

What in the world does that mean? How can a person improve? This is way too subjective. When you say something like that to an employee, you could be attacking self-esteem. A person's attitude is attached to who she is. You say, "Pat, you have a bad attitude," and in Pat's brain it translates to, "Pat, you are a

No one is "always" anything.

bad person." No — you didn't say that, but that's what Pat hears. Think about it. If someone says to you, "Work on your attitude," what is your internal response? You become defensive, don't you? If you want openness between you and the people on your team, stop talking about attitudes. Instead, talk about behavior. If you want to change attitudes, that's where to start. Why? Because you can't modify other people's attitudes. You can only modify behavior.

Assume the Employee Knows the Problem and Solution

You hurt the performance of your team whenever you assume the employee knows both the problem and the solution. Assuming invariably costs time, money and morale. There are a few assumptions, however, that are excellent for you to make as a coach.

- Assume that your communications were somehow inadequate the first time. Then follow the ΛBCs of ensuring understanding.

    Ask the employee what she thinks you want or said.

    Blame no one if that understanding is wrong.

    Communicate more clearly … then
    confirm comprehension.

- Assume that your employee can learn to do anything, that she has the potential. Realistically you may need to temper your decisions with the fact that, for some people, improvement is indeed possible, just not in this lifetime.

- Assume that people do want to learn and grow and excel. The positive attitude gives you the benefit of being open, regardless.

> *"All we pay for every week is a certain kind of behavior for a certain amount of hours and that's the only thing we can modify."*
>
> — Ferdinand Fournies

2

Never Follow Up

If you fail to follow up on directions or performance, you will inevitably find yourself reacting to unpleasant surprises.

Example: Let's say you gave an assignment to someone on Monday and it's due on Friday. You say, "I need this on Friday morning for a meeting." Friday morning comes and you ask the assigned person, "Where's that information you were going to give me this morning for the meeting?" The person looks at you and says, "I forgot" or "It's not done yet." If you're a yeller, you yell. If you're a crier, you cry. But who is really to blame? You are! You didn't follow up.

A crucial part of following up is setting objectives.

Example: You give someone an assignment on Monday morning. As you hand her the assignment you say, "By Wednesday, the first draft should be done. By Thursday, the rewritten version should be done, and by Friday morning, the whole thing should be completed." Then you follow up. You check on Wednesday to see if the project is on schedule. Then you check on Thursday. If for some reason the project isn't where it's supposed to be, you and your employee can then do the following:

1. Pinpoint what is preventing project flow (job overload, lack of information, mind block, etc.).

2. Eliminate the impediment (reassign conflicting work, brainstorm solutions, provide helpful materials, etc.).

3. Determine how to get back on schedule (overtime, involvement of others, extended completion date).

Caution: Make sure you communicate that you're not doing this to control, but to follow up so that the responsible person gets the best results.

Example

"Let's just roll up our sleeves and tackle the problem together, Deb. I know you are as anxious as I am to do the project well and I want to see you succeed."

Once you have implemented this procedure one or two times with a team member, watch the awareness dawn on her and note how she deals with future projects!

A crucial part of following up is setting objectives.

2

Don't Reward Improved Behavior

If you don't reward positive changes in behavior, your team will be defeated. You will not gain permanent behavior changes. Every performance improvement, however small, needs some type of reward. Behavioral scientists continually study motivation, and, as Dr. Rollo May has taught, the greatest secret for performance is that what gets rewarded gets repeated. The top two things that consistently motivate people are achievement and recognition. Maslow's hierarchy and Herzberg's cautions of dissatisfiers both place recognition and achievement on the highest rungs of behavioral cause.

If people feel they're achieving something, they are motivated. If you go through your day and feel as if you're getting nothing done, how do you feel at the end of that day? Wasted. But if you go through your day and get a lot accomplished, you feel great! You're motivated. Similarly, when people are recognized for their achievement, they feel motivated. Take 10 to 20 minutes at either the beginning or end of every week and sit down with your team. In that meeting, review what they've accomplished the last week. Recognize individuals. Tell them how much you appreciate what Gale has done or what Pat did today. When you do this, you're setting up your team to be motivated for the following week.

> *Every performance improvement, however small, deserves some type of reward.*

2

Case Study

Raytown Kennels employs 12 people: one office manager, two clerical support people, two welders, two delivery people, two kennel maintenance people, one trainer, one veterinarian and one communications manager.

Barb Smith, the office manager, is also the owner of the business. Last fall, when the hunting season was in full swing, the business was faced with an unusually large demand for new kennels and doghouses. The welders could not keep up with requests.

Barb called a meeting and announced that everyone except the clerical support people would be taught how to construct kennels in two late-night training sessions. The welders were to provide the training. All were required to attend these sessions — no exceptions — because, as Barb put it, "The future of the business and everyone's job is on the line."

During the next 60 days, more than 30 kennel orders were filled on time. However, eight of them were returned or delivery was declined because of construction flaws or design errors. And the much-respected company veterinarian resigned to take a job with a competitor.

At a company picnic in the spring, Barb gave a short speech in which she thanked all in attendance for their loyalty during the last year and promised to avoid a repeat of "the fiasco of last fall" through better sales projections and production planning.

She closed by announcing that a new veterinary graduate (her nephew) would be joining the company in June.

1. What pitfalls to StaffCoaching™ success did Barb fall into?

2. What did she do right?

3. Briefly describe how Barb could have avoided the pitfalls you listed under No. 1.

4. If you were one of Barb's people, how would you feel about working for her?

5. What one thing could Barb Smith do to immediately remedy the major problem(s) you see in her organization?

Case Analysis

Several things that could have been avoided seem to jump out in this case.

First, Barb did not have access to backup staff or specialists who could meet her production demand. Although it seemed like a good idea to cross-train her people in kennel construction, the obvious dissatisfaction of some employees is noted. Barb could have avoided much of this difficulty by identifying free-lance welders or outside resources to contact when welding demands

**C
A
S
E

S
T
U
D
Y**

rise. It's also a good idea to cover her delivery people and support staff. It is cost-ineffective for veterinary staff to weld kennels or deliver products.

Second, the tone and atmosphere of Barb's decision seems questionable. Did her people enter into the plan? Were they willing volunteers meeting a business need or were they commanded to perform? Strong-arm tactics may lead to compliance but not necessarily quality work.

Third, Barb did not provide adequate incentive in the training. Reading the case makes an individual wonder why employees would give up their time and do work that is not within their job descriptions.

Last, Barb did not inspect or maintain any form of quality control, losing the most valuable resource she had, her customer loyalty. One alternative for Barb would have been to assign her welders as inspectors and quality-assurance monitors.

Ten Tools to Ensure Team Results

An excellent coach focuses on the team performance, realizing that the whole is greater that any of its parts. There are 10 tools available to you to give you a foundation for more fully developing the values that are beneficial to you as a coach. These tools not only strengthen your ability to initiate change on the part of your team, but also stimulate the trust and rapport necessary for coaching to be effective. These tools facilitate all your interactions.

These tools are important elements of successful StaffCoaching™: They aid you in deciding how to build a solid team foundation.

These are proven attributes of a successful StaffCoach™ that guarantee your success with your team. Consider your own style as you study each.

1. Flexibility
2. Helping
3. Empathy and Understanding
4. Valuing the Employee

5. Listening

6. "Proactive" Mindset

7. Effective Feedback

8. Enthusiasm and Optimism

9. Openness

10. Humor

Flexibility

If you've been in your job awhile, chances are you could have a tendency toward laxity, lethargy … toward "routine." And if a coach is stuck in a rut, it could mean more rigidity in a leadership style. As a coach, you may find the team is less successful. Flexibility allows you to see change as a positive. It encourages creativity and an openness for diversity.

Whenever you get a new team member, when someone on the team has a new responsibility, if someone leaves, or a new customer enters the picture, you have a change. The most successful coaches are people who are flexible in responding to these developments. They use different team strategies to succeed. What's an easy way to remain flexible? Being committed to personal growth makes you a perfect role model for the people you must mentor.

Helping

The willingness to work shoulder to shoulder with your team in accomplishing goals … assisting in any way you can … happens only as a result of your attitude. As the leader, you exist to help the people who work for you. That should be your professional mission. All too often, leaders don't think that way. They think that because they are leaders, their people are supposed to be helping them. Sorry. Not true. The true role of the effective coach is to assist team members in their successful efforts to further department and company goals.

> *The longer you're in a job, the more rigid you become.*

> *Personal growth is the only guaranteed rut-preventer!*

Empathy and Understanding

To succeed as a coach, you must have empathy for the people who work for you — a basic understanding and acceptance of human nature. People are people. If you expect people to be super-beings or pawns in a corporate ladder-climbing game, there is little chance you will be able to inspire them to greater heights. People aren't enthusiastic about being with someone who lacks sensitivity toward them or their situation.

To help you maintain a proper "people perspective," many managers have found these "Five Golden Questions for Leading People" to be helpful.

1. Have I communicated the assignment in a way that makes my employee feel she must "do or die"?

2. Do my instructions sound like marching orders, or like helpful directions toward a mutually desired destination?

3. Can my employee excel if she completes this assignment, or is it possible only to do "just what's expected"?

4. If I had to perform this task that I am assigning, would I look forward to doing it for a boss like me?

5. Does my employee believe that I understand her frustrations, or do I appear mistake-proof, regret-proof … feeling-proof?

Valuing the Employee

A team can't function at its best unless it feels valuable.

A team can't function at its best unless it feels valuable. That feeling can come only from you, as you provide encouragement and opportunities for increased individual success. If individuals on your team slowly get the feeling that the results of their efforts are somehow more important than they are, success will plummet. On the other hand, if you are each person's biggest fan … each person's most ardent supporter … you'll see results you never would have expected.

For example, find something complimentary to say to the individual(s) who performed a newly completed task. Even if the job turned out badly, a supportive coach finds something positive to say. Make it a rule, therefore, to find something about the completed job that does at least one of the following:

- Reflects a unique attribute of the employee(s) who performed the task

  "Lynn, I could see your special eye for detail in the presentation materials!"

  — or —

- Verifies your feeling that the employee(s) were right for the project

  "Kim, I knew I could count on you to meet or beat the deadline, and you were two days early!"

  — or —

- Makes the team even better than before

  "Thanks to you, Terry, they'll know what department to bring this kind of challenge to in the future."

Listening

Too many coaches believe that what they say is more important than what they hear — and that listening to team members is an effortless or passive aspect of the communication process. The model of "I talk, you listen; you talk, I listen" is wrong. It's a much more lopsided process. The majority of effective communication is spent in listening behaviors — and truly good listening requires conscious effort. Failure to understand those two key facts can cause you to misread team members' intentions, jump to incorrect conclusions and, ultimately, antagonize your people.

Effective coaches become students of listening, and the very best ones consistently practice the following five principles of listening:

> *At least half of effective communication is listening.*

1. **Listen to what the speaker is saying.**

   Do you understand what was said well enough to write it down? If not, ask questions.

2. **Listen to what is meant.**

   Does the speaker's tone contradict the words (i.e., sarcasm) … does she "load" the words to sell a point of view?

   "I think we should buy the new system — especially if we have to meet the quotas you forecast."

3. **"Listen" to the speaker's body language.**

   You don't have to be a psychologist to benefit from the full message your team member sends as she speaks verbally and nonverbally. For instance:

   (a) Is her facial expression (smile) inconsistent with other nonverbal clues (clenched fists)?

   (b) Are gestures saying something that words alone cannot (i.e., tapping fingers revealing boredom, nodding head to communicate understanding, scratching head in confusion)?

   (c) Does the person's posture suggest special meaning (i.e., slumped wearily in chair … seated fearfully on chair edge … pacing the floor while talking)?

4. **Monitor your own nonverbal messages.**

   Does your use of eye contact show genuine interest? Or do you look as if you're preparing a response while the person is still speaking? Or, equally bad, are you checking your watch during the conversation?

5. **Ask yourself, "Can team members who talk to me expect empathy … or judgment?"**

   Never give people the feeling that you have prejudged their communications. Your respect for a team member's ideas and feelings builds up her esteem … even if you ultimately disagree with her opinion. But, when you show disagreement even before she has "made a case," you risk wounding ego and self-esteem that may never fully recover.

Does your use of eye contact show genuine interest?

Listening like a coach is a very critical, very necessary business. The manual, *Learn to Listen*, by Jim Dugger, National Press Publications, explains the different ways that people listen and the necessity of perfecting this little taught skill.

"Proactive" Mindset

Another key to effective coaching is to be "proactive." An effective coach doesn't wait for things to happen. She makes them happen. Are you introducing new ideas ... new solutions? Or do they happen only as a reaction to problems? A proactive coach beats problems to the punch!

Example

Claire:

Hi, Pat. What are you looking for in here?

Coach:

Oh, hi, Claire. I was just wondering if taking this wall out would make it easier for computer designers to get to the copier room?

Claire:

I never thought about that. Wow! They have to go clear around and through the break room to get here now.

Coach:

I know. And they use this color copier three times more than anyone on the floor.

Claire:

They will love you if you do that.

Coach:

Well, I think I better check first and see if the building maintenance people would love the idea. But it sure seems as if it would make sense.

In this example, Pat is looking for ways to make her staff's jobs easier. Although she cannot yet promise that a wall can be removed, she is thinking about how people can do their jobs better and more effectively. Notice also that Pat has not overpromised and is thinking about the ramifications of her actions. Good ideas often come with a price tag that must be measured before a manager jumps in.

Make it a daily habit to encourage your people.

Effective Feedback

Coaching effectively requires you to develop strong feedback skills. Learn how to let people know when they've done a good job or when they need to correct their course. Praise and critiques are kinds of feedback. Make it a daily habit to encourage your people … to assure them that they are the focus of your professional life … with regular feedback. Like listening skills, feedback demands practice until it becomes second nature.

The following chart lists some opportunities for feedback and some suggested methods for doing it. As you read, build on this list and add other methods for acknowledging performance.

Opportunities for Feedback	Feedback Method
Successful project completion	Team meeting to praise the group and acknowledge special individual effort Congratulatory note to all involved
Individual accomplishment	One-on-one meeting commending performance Letter to upper management acknowledging the individual's performance (with copy to employee)
Project in progress	Meet to review and report on progress. • Analyze problems so far. • Anticipate upcoming challenges. • Praise achievement (individual and group).
Rumor concerning organizational or project change	Meeting, e-mail or memo acknowledging the rumor, either confirming or refuting the rumor, point by point.
Project failure	Team or individual meeting 1. Analyze what went wrong. 2. Discuss what was learned. 3. Decide what to do differently next time. 4. Reaffirm coach's faith in team and individual ability. 5. Spotlight individual accomplishments (if any).

Enthusiasm and Optimism

The tools of enthusiasm and a positive outlook are communicated to a team primarily through the manager's choice of language. Note when you ask, "How are you doing? How was lunch?" Keep interest in your voice so it doesn't sound like a rhetorical question that generates immense surprise if someone actually responds. Common language responses communicate apathy, lassitude and lack of interest. Go beyond routine responses to get better results — change your language. Use words like "outstanding," "wonderful," "excellent," "great," "fantastic," "terrific." Start using words that go beyond the norm and watch what happens. You'll have a different attitude toward the commonplace.

The team will respond when you walk into a room if you watch and respond to their expressions, postures and attitudes. Their backs will straighten, the corners of their mouths will turn up, and they will unconsciously reflect your positive spirit in spite of themselves. But here's the best news. Managers who have tested upbeat language in the workplace report that after a while, just entering the office or building will produce the same effect!

Enthusiasm and optimism are also expressed in how you describe a situation or explain a job. Going beyond the norm or emphasizing the positives can affect the team's approach to the task. Face it, as a coach, you set the mood.

In case you think it's wrong to say you feel great when you don't or act like you do when you don't, understand this: If you ask the nation's most successful coaches how they are doing any day of the week, they'll tell you "great, wonderful, terrific, excellent." Why? Because they are choosing their attitudes. They are choosing how they feel and how they want the team to feel.

Openness

Another key to effective coaching is to be nonproprietary. This means not holding things back from your team members to retain a power position. Be open in how you feel or what your reaction is to a situation. Certainly there are informational areas restricted to managers. But withholding information that enables a team

> *Use words like "outstanding," "wonderful," "excellent," "great," "fantastic," "terrific."*

member to do her tasks more efficiently … maybe even replace you at some point in the future … is not protecting your job. It is jeopardizing it!

Example

Phil:

You want me to present the specs on the project?

Coach:

I think you would be the perfect supervisor to do it. Your crew worked hardest at finding a solution, you put in more hours …

Phil:

But, Kathleen, it's your design idea. You came up with it.

Coach:

I may have put the period on the sentence, but a lot of team brainstorming made the words possible. Besides, you are better on your feet than I am.

Phil:

Even if that were true … which it isn't … my point is that they'll think my crew came up with the idea.

Coach:

Then set them straight. Tell them our entire team did it. And tell them we are proud of the total effort that went into the discovery for the organization's sake.

When your people learn to trust you for tips and techniques that make them more valuable, your own value … to them and to the company … is compounded! Share the wealth and your wealth will grow.

Humor

Humor in the workplace is the No. 1 stress buster. It is also the best way to connect. Can your people laugh with you … even at you … without risking retribution? No work environment is less appealing than one that bans or discourages humor. Make humor a welcome and honored co-worker every day of the week. When

> *Share the wealth and your wealth will grow.*

Laugh at your weaknesses and you'll never run out of things to laugh about.

people laugh, their mistakes and setbacks are easier to tolerate and more easily overcome.

Humor … especially when it comes from the top down … communicates a calming message that permeates the very fabric of a team. The message is: People aren't perfect and we don't expect it. Humor suggests an informal, people-focused organization where individuals on a team matter and where innovation is valued. In a wonderful way, humor acknowledges that we are all in the same leaky boat together, bailing out the water as fast as we can. Sure, our boat will make it from shore A to shore B, but only because we are a well-knit team. And only because we bail the "leaks" with humor!

When was the last time a surprise "over the hill" party was given for someone in your group? How about a "dubious achievement" award (i.e., an "I'm allergic to Mondays" poster)? Have you had a pizza party during the lunch hour where admittance requires the individual to tell a joke upon entering? Do you encourage play? Your team needs your endorsement in order to set in motion the freeing element of humor!

Edwin Whipple said, "Wherever you find humor, you find compassion close by." It won't happen without your help, so let your team know you endorse humor. More than a character trait, humor is an art that requires practice.

Case Study

After two years of concept development and testing … plus several presentations … Charlotte Dunn obtained an SBA loan to produce a line of specialty posters. Key to getting the loan was the fact that she already owned and operated a moderately profitable poster line directed to the teen-age market. The new line was to be targeted to adults for offices and homes and would be sold over the Internet.

With the loan money, Charlotte added four new people to her eight-person staff and retained a new sales rep team to market her products. Unlike the posters Charlotte marketed to teens, the new adult posters had no words, only pictures. Some were scenic, some were abstract, but all communicated a fine-art feel … at poster prices. Limited testing revealed support for Charlotte's idea.

Charlotte worked long hours side by side with her graphic team, then with the printing crew, to produce a quantity of her new posters in time for the spring New York retail sales convention. When it looked as if the posters might not be finished on time, Charlotte brought a toy whip to work and laughingly "cracked" it throughout the office for several days. When the deadline was met, she presented everyone with a customized poster that read, "(Employee name) didn't have to be crazy to come to work here, but it helped!" Beneath the words was a photo of Charlotte cracking her toy whip.

Sales at the convention were dismal. Orders from the Web and in response to direct-mail catalog sheets were no better. Telemarketing efforts to help reps stimulate retail interest generated very little success. Finally, three of Charlotte's oldest employees came to her and suggested adding copy to the new posters. They said they had always felt uneasy about the wordless posters. They had always felt the idea was wrong for the market, in spite of the local focus-group tests. Charlotte slept on it and finally agreed.

During the next two weeks, she and her team ran the entire new poster inventory through a sheet-fed press and printed quotes, poetry and song lyrics onto every design. Charlotte discovered that even the poster pictures on her remaining inventory of catalog sheets could be overprinted with the new copy. And, because the backs of the sheets were blank, she could imprint store addresses (along with a discount offer) … then simply fold, stamp and mail to her market. Then Charlotte and the team members who suggested the revisions flew to New York and presented the new posters to the sales rep team.

Sales crept steadily upward during the summer and fall, then jumped nicely during the holiday-buying season. The results? Charlotte's team lost only 11 percent of projected sales on the new line. And, since the teen poster line had exceeded projections by 12 percent, the firm was 1 percent in the black!

At a special dinner party for "The One-Percent Gang," Charlotte announced plans to establish a "New Idea Review Committee" made up of employee-elected team members whose goal would be to develop, test and approve new product ideas —

and to "keep crazy business owners from doing their own thing." Then Charlotte presented everyone with a $1,000 bonus check ... postdated one year from that day ... explaining, "The dollars aren't there now, but in one year ... with a team like you ... it's money in the bank!"

Case Study Analysis

1. As a StaffCoach™, what would you have done differently in making plans to expand?

2. What do you think Charlotte's natural StaffCoach™ style is: counselor, mentor or coach? Why?

3. Next to each of the 10 tools for building a solid team foundation, grade Charlotte from one to 10 — ten being the highest — and give a brief reason for your grade.

    *   Flexibility

    *   Helping

    *   Empathy and understanding

    *   Valuing the employee

    *   Listening

    *   Proactive mindset

    *   Effective feedback

- Enthusiasm and optimism

- Openness

- Humor

4. What was the biggest thing Charlotte did right as a StaffCoach™? What was her most glaring mistake?

5. What StaffCoach™ attribute exhibited by Charlotte would be especially welcomed by your team? How could you take steps to develop that attribute?

A recovery plan like Charlotte's indicates the ability to learn from one's mistakes. Although this did not end in total disaster, unless something is done differently in the future, this will occur again, and sales may not bounce back as strong.

One concern that appears to be left unaddressed is the lack of negative feedback from her staff. Especially in new product development, seasoned staff members must learn to speak up and discuss their concerns, not nod and see if something flies. This could have been a costly mistake. Charlotte needs to address why only three people spoke up and then only after near disaster. Rather than looking to the staff, she needs to really look inside: What is she doing to stifle honesty?

On the positive side, the atmosphere around Charlotte's project seems positive and engaging. She truly demonstrated an awareness of the production slippage and how to get people engaged to meet the deadline. The fact that she used humor and then rewarded her team makes hard work much more palatable.

Summary

Coaching is a process. It includes distinct approaches — inspiring, teaching and correcting. The benefit of the StaffCoach™ Model is that it gives you a guide to change roles as your people require. Use the coaching role when your staff's performance is average, act as a mentor when performance is above average, and counsel when performance is below average.

To make sure you choose an approach based on need and not habit or preference, take the style inventory and learn your strengths and biases in terms of each role. This awareness and knowledge of the other pitfalls to coaching can accelerate your ability to support and grow your staff. Likewise, regularly assess your inner tools, sharpening those attributes that are equated with successful team management.

Chapter Quiz

1. What is the first step in the Five-Step StaffCoaching™ Model?

2. What are four ways to determine an employee's performance level?

3. Why is knowing your StaffCoaching™ style important?

4. Name the ABCs of ensuring employee understanding.

5. List the six pitfalls to StaffCoaching™ success.

CHAPTER 3

The Coaching Role: Inspiring and Motivating

Catch people doing something right.

History buffs will agree that a prime example of coaching is Henry Kaiser, an industrialist. He thought possibilities continually surpassed what others thought couldn't be done. Historians attribute winning World War II to his inspiring and motivating management of shipbuilding crews. He took ordinary people who thought it took three months to build a ship and said, "Fine, give me one in four-and-a-half days." Instead of monetary rewards, he broke his workers into teams and had them compete with each other. When told there wasn't enough steel for the ships, he built the first Pacific steel plant. When told there wasn't enough magnesium, he built a magnesium plant. His teams produced 1,466 ships for the war effort. He led a consortium of builders and constructed Hoover Dam in two years, under schedule. Average performers and extraordinary results!

Coaching is more than a set of management actions for improving performance. It is an involved and supportive approach for allowing others to realize their potential. Coaching is a partnership, as Kaiser demonstrated, for achieving results. Both he and his production teams played vital parts.

Coaching rests more on motivation and interpersonal influence than on getting others to comply through a chain of command or hierarchy. Jack Welch and GE's decentralized mega-organization illustrate this. Coaching isn't a mechanical

> *"A good coach is not necessarily a winner but a person who is a good teacher … who doesn't abuse his or her players … who gets the most from the players and who works within the framework of the rules."*
>
> — Dan Devine

3

process between the coach and individual or team; it requires good chemistry, a lot of listening and observing — and caring. Barbara Jordan exudes that caring, whether she is in front of an audience, beside a group of citizens or among her staff.

As a StaffCoach™, you will use all three approaches — coaching, mentoring and counseling — as your people need them. For the people who do average work, meet all their goals and handle their accountabilities, you will get the best results from coaching them. Help them directly improve their performance and go beyond "just enough."

Coaching is at the heart of the StaffCoach™ Model. Its actions are the foundation for mentoring and counseling. The guidelines, steps and techniques apply to all. Whenever you want to move your people, get buy-in, inspire or motivate, coaching is the answer.

The Coaching Role

Coaching is a before, during and after set of activities. It goes beyond the game and throughout your people's employment. It's not a single action. You won't be able to review an employee's past performance, note that he has been doing just enough to get by — no more, no less — and decide this guy needs some coaching. Since you have five minutes you call him in, give him a "one more for the old gipper" speech and shove him out the door with a friendly pat on the shoulder and an "I know you can do it" farewell. This may be abdicating or copping out, but it sure isn't coaching.

Your role as a coach involves basic, continuous facilitation.

1. **Involvement and trust**

    Your overall relationship, just like a preseason, is devoted to communicating your willingness and ability to support the team. Immersing yourself in their activities and interests and involving them in discussions is a trust-builder, for both sides. As tasks occur, just as a regular season of play arrives, team members should be convinced that you are the right coach for them … even if your decisions aren't always popular. You and the team are

80

together, learning about each other and how you can rely on each other.

2. Clarifying and verifying

Before any job, just as before every game, you "clarify" expectations for your team by reviewing the desired outcome, what's expected, the game plan. This includes letting them know how you keep score. Measurements are a part of clarification as well as instruments for motivation and accomplishment. It's a form of "no secrets, no surprises" style of management. You "verify" the team's understanding by asking each team member to explain his special assignment(s) during specific tasks, like game situations. Speaking doesn't guarantee that they get it. Test their understanding of what they think are the results and restrictions. Clarify the goals and objectives to verify that they understand.

3. Affirming and acknowledging

You observe the performance of your people. You acknowledge team members, giving them special reminders, warnings, encouragement and praise. You acknowledge the team by your visible, vocal, and tactical involvement and support. Credible affirmation relies on your knowledge of your people. The question isn't whether or not they want recognition; it's how they prefer to be recognized. Effective coaching underlines every excellent behavior and notes each step forward — so that it gets repeated. In order to make sure your people listen to you and really hear you, affirm them individually.

4. Motivating and inspiring

In sports, when a time-out is called just before the tie-breaking point is played, the coach reminds team members what is at stake … what rewards await the individuals who make the winning team effort. As a manager, you challenge team members with the memory of past victories, with examples of what they accomplished. You enthuse, you excite, you encourage — so they believe they can do it. Motivating and inspiring are about them, not you. It's about instilling the confidence and energy that has them achieving the results. It's what causes ownership.

These actions of the coaching role of the StaffCoach™ are self-perpetuating. As people become motivated, they trust, which reinforces what they can and should do. This affirms that they are doing the right things, which in turn motivates.

This personalized and focused attention takes your employee and your team to optimum behaviors. You move people from an average, okay performance to greater gains.

The Coach's Role in Communicating Involvement and Establishing Trust

Critical to your ability to function effectively in the coaching role are your willingness and ability to:

1. Become involved with your team.

2. Develop trust.

While the two work very closely together, there are differences.

Your Involvement as a Coach

In Chapter 1, the 10 values of a successful Staff Coach™ stated that the coach's involvement in team activities is perceived by team members as "caring." Management expert Tom Peters came up with a concept called "MBWA: Management by Walking Around." This means simply being with the members of your team. It means getting out from behind your desk … being available … asking questions about people and projects. How are your people doing? Can you help? Is there something you can do to improve a process? Peters asks an important question: How can you coach what you don't know, see and understand?

The more you get involved with your team members, the easier it is to express something to them in a meaningful way. If you know what they are dealing with, their frustrations and the skills they use, then you will be able to pinpoint exactly what they need to change. It's harder for someone to listen to you and your encouragement or advice if they doubt you really know what's going on. Until you establish that you are savvy to the work and their way of doing it, you won't get results.

Think for a moment about the bosses who have made the greatest impact on your life. There are undoubtedly positive things you can say about each memorable boss. For instance, you might be able to say that he:

1. Was the one who taught me the value of _____.

2. Encouraged me the most by _____.

3. Consistently exhibited the admirable quality of

_____.

There may be negative remarks you could make about the same bosses. But it's the impact on you that equates with coaching success. Additionally, there was probably one other statement you could make about that boss, a statement that makes all the others meaningful. That statement is this:

> *"(Boss's name) cared about who I was, what I thought and what I aspired to."*

Understanding why you are involved is important. This relates back to why you get paid. Think about it. While coaching is all about getting results, you aren't paid for what YOU do, you're paid for what your associates do! Managing is getting results from others. You need your employees and that team. Involvement leads to understanding, rapport, credibility and trust.

Developing Trust

Developing trust among team members and between the coach and each individual is crucial. It is an outcome of involvement. Without trust, your people won't take you or your support seriously. They may think you are a great person, but just not one who knows how tough their jobs are or the way things really are. It is more than being able to rely on each other and know each is there for the other. That's important, but trust is more: It's knowing that each of you can do what is needed in the relationship.

Trust is built by laying critical foundation stones.

> *Trust is built by laying critical foundation stones.*

3

• **Confidentiality**

In order to push the individual to the next level, you must know his weaknesses and fears as well as his strengths and motives. Why would he confide in you unless there was a sense of privacy? The moment you repeat something told to you in confidence, you risk the loss of mutual trust.

To illustrate this point for yourself, complete this short exercise, answering candidly in light of the information provided.

You are in a private meeting with your brand-new boss, briefing him on the status of the work group you supervise. You are the third of four supervisors he has met with today. During the course of your conversation, he comments to you that 1) he probably wouldn't have taken this job if the salary wasn't "top dollar," and 2) the supervisor just before you apparently "has a problem at home that occupies too much of his thinking."

In response to the questions, check the boxes true or false.

I would not hesitate to tell this new boss my personal problems.	❑ T	❑ F
I believe my new boss is fully committed to company goals and employee development.	❑ T	❑ F
I can be completely confident that my new boss will not talk about me behind my back.	❑ T	❑ F
Just because my boss gossiped a little doesn't mean I can't trust him in other areas.	❑ T	❑ F
When the job gets long and the task hard, I know the uncompromising character of my boss will provide needed inspiration.	❑ T	❑ F

Did you answer all five "false"? Of course. That's because the word "false" always becomes associated (consciously or unconsciously) with betrayals of confidence … especially at the coach level! If you learn only one lesson from this manual, learn to fight the urge to look important by telling all you know! That one truth alone is worth a whole library of books like this one.

- **Supporting your team members**

   Let them know that, right or wrong, you rise or fall with them. If every member believes you will support him in the daily performance of team duties, your team will respond to your goals. Support is tied to synergy. As soon and as fast as you can get across that you win when they win, you begin knitting together and as a unit are able to accomplish more. It requires confidence, and that requires knowledge.

- **Rewarding performance**

   Use rewards generously. Remember, what gets rewarded gets repeated. Rewards run a spectrum from promotions, raises or bonuses to a day off, bowling or lunch, to complimenting him or giving him a sticker of merit or a humorous "award." They don't have to be monetary. Praise can be one of the most important of all rewards when properly used.

   Here are five keys to making praise a valuable reward for good performance.

   1. Praise only when it is truly deserved, not to pump up an employee. Overpraising, or praising a ridiculous action, has a ring of insincerity that fools no one.

   2. Criticize in private, compliment in public. When employees make a mistake, they should never be admonished publicly. Praise anytime, anywhere.

   3. Don't assume that people would be embarrassed with praise. Be sensitive to their personalities and choose the time and place with that in mind. Recognition and praise are a way to honor them.

> *"I don't care how great, how famous or successful a man or woman may be, each hungers for applause."*
>
> — George M. Adams

4. Avoid praising one individual or group in hopes of boosting performance in another. This kind of manipulation is easily spotted. Competition doesn't motivate everybody.

5. You don't have to wait for major accomplishments to offer praise. Rewarding small achievements with praise is a great way to shape behavior.

   In Bob Nelson's book, *1001 Ways to Reward Employees*, rewards include positive reinforcement, motivational strategy, appreciation, recognition or just common courtesy. Recognition fosters job satisfaction, builds self-esteem and reinforces desired performance.

- **Honesty**

   Humorist Kim Hubbard said, "Honesty pays, but it don't seem to pay enough to suit some people." For a coach, however, it definitely pays the bills. Nothing is more evident to team members than lack of honesty at the management level. You can't hide dishonesty, even when it is "in the best interests" of employees. Without honesty, there can't be the trust and confidence inherent in any relationship.

   Example

   Mike Riley's production team is divided into three highly competitive shifts, each working the same assembly line process. About two months ago, Mike kicked off a contest that is one day away from completion. The three teams are neck and neck in a competition for output-per-hour leadership. The winning team will be the guest of the other two teams at a huge barbecue dinner and dance.

   About an hour ago, Mike was told that the automotive part produced by his competing teams was discontinued six days ago.

   Mike's choices are the following:

1. Allow the contest to continue. Don't disappoint team members by telling them they have worked all this time on a discontinued part. Wait until after the barbecue awards dinner.

3

2. Allow the contest to continue. Don't tell team members at all. If anyone finds out, tell the truth: You didn't want to disappoint them.

3. Halt the contest. Announce the part discontinuance. Tally the results of the contest so far and declare a winner based on output to date.

Example Analysis

At this point, you may be saying, "Hey, what difference does it make? It wasn't Mike's fault. This can't be a big deal one way or the other." Can't it? Think about it.

In this instance, team morale is definitely at stake. Nearly two months of work would be for nothing. Additionally, if competition is very close, calling the contest one day early could penalize a team that believes it has a full day to "catch up." What might the effect be for other contests?

Further, the unfortunate fact is that the bearer of bad news is often seen in a negative light. Some might question if Mike knew all along. Blameless or not, Mike is not going to be greeted with smiles at his announcement. In fact, for the next several months he could be hearing "are you sure?" every time he assigns a new production schedule.

There's no way around it. The critical issue here is honesty, as it is in any situation where you have a truth that affects the team. Can your team count on you to "bite the bullet" and level with them at all costs? Or are they going to always wonder if you are withholding some information on every project in order to spare their feelings? Taking an "easy way out" never works for a coach.

Tell your people the truth, even if it hurts. They will learn they can depend on you to shoot straight with them — and they will reciprocate. Honesty is part of honoring and respect.

- **Encouraging communication freedom**

    You've heard the expression, "My door is always open," yet the reality often is open door, closed mind. Regardless, your team should be absolutely convinced that it is the

> *Tell your people the truth, even if it hurts.*

figurative truth. When your team trusts you with any news … personal or professional … and expects you to hear with objectivity, understanding and compassion, you are a coach who can count on the "extra mile" from your people. Your team has to know that you are accessible to them.

How do you know if you are providing communication freedom?

Check if you really do have communication freedom with these 10 questions.

1. Do my people feel free to disagree with me when we talk?

2. Are team members aware of the basic problems I have to cope with in coaching them?

3. Am I able to tell any team member when he misses the mark — without putting him down?

4. Do my people know at least two specific things they can do to get a better rating at the next performance review?

5. Do my team members know I understand their personal goals?

6. Are my people aware of the major decisions I have made this year in coaching them?

7. Do I coach my people toward improvement when they need it?

8. Do team members understand exactly what I expect of them?

9. Do I acknowledge the good things accomplished by each of my people?

10. Can my people ask for help at any time without feeling embarrassed?

If you can answer "yes" to at least eight of these 10 questions, then you are well on the way to measurable StaffCoach™ success!

- **Consistency**

    If you are a leader who tends to be impulsive, or if you
    have high highs.and low lows, hear these words of
    warning: Your inconsistencies can make your people
    paranoid. You will have great difficulty taking people to
    higher levels of performance if they're not sure that what
    you want is what you want.

    ### Example

    Sean has a longstanding department rule: Plans to
    take vacation days in conjunction with major holidays
    must be submitted to the office manager at least 90
    days in advance.

    With Christmas only three weeks away, his most
    productive telesales agent, Jim, notified Sean that he
    wanted to take four vacation days the week after
    Christmas to be with his fiancée in California. After much
    inner turmoil, Sean reluctantly agreed.

    Two days later, Sean's least productive telesales agent
    approached him with a similar request. Sean told him
    about the department rule.

    "But you let Jim go," the employee pointed out quickly.
    "And I've been here longer than he has."

    What should Sean have done?

    ### Example Analysis

    It's more a question of what he shouldn't have done. If a
    reasonable rule is established for good, profit-related
    reasons, it should be obeyed, barring unforeseen family
    emergencies, etc.

    Naturally, if the rule isn't reasonable, it should be
    abolished. In this case, Sean allowed a rule to be broken
    because the rule breaker was a recognized good performer.
    But do you see the can of worms he has opened? Do you
    see the message he is communicating to his team: Rules
    are rules until I say they aren't? That will be a hard
    message for Sean to live down.

3

Sit down and think through your decisions. If necessary, involve another manager you admire in order to make sure that you are thinking logically and that you can follow through on future policies related to the decision. Inconsistencies can be sidestepped with a little up-front patience and planning — but, once committed, they are extremely difficult to overcome.

And, check out all those rules. Many rules were established for the convenience of the boss or organization. Today's workforce wants fair and realistic standards and will question anything that appears illogical.

The Coach's Role in Clarifying Expectations and Verifying Understanding

You can't expect to have an impact on people without involvement and trust. The first thing you must do to achieve results, however, is clarify goals. Tom Gilbert, the father of performance management, teaches that you always describe what good performance looks like and let employees know how you will measure successes.

The finest game plan for the best team won't guarantee success unless that plan is communicated and understood. That's why coaches of professional athletes spend so much time reviewing and discussing game films, designing play books, conducting "chalk talks," diagramming sideline plays, etc. Many coaches believe that the game is won or lost before the actual competition, depending on how well the game plan has been presented and understood by team members.

The same holds true for the military, business and industry, and any project management. There is no question that victories in the organizational environment cannot happen without clear, purposeful direction from the StaffCoach™ and consistent team member comprehension. You can still fail despite having those key elements, through factors beyond your control (e.g., policy changes, equipment or material altcrations, inadequate or incorrect information). But probability says that the clearer the goal, the surer the achievement.

3

One of the biggest challenges faced by managers is to get employees to do what they are supposed to do. Coaches have the additional challenge of getting employees to do more than what they are supposed to do. While working as a management consultant, Ferdinand Fournies collected information from more than 20,000 managers and discovered that there are 16 specific reasons why employees do not do what they're supposed to do. The top three reasons follow:

1. They don't know what they are supposed to do.

2. They don't know why they are supposed to do it.

3. They don't know how to do it.

Each of these causes of nonperformance can be addressed immediately with the StaffCoach™ Model. The coach tells them the "what" — setting expectations and showing them how to know when they achieve them. The mentor handles the why and the counselor deals with the how.

How do you start any coaching session to establish the "what"?

Clarify Your Expectations as Coach: How to Say What You Think You Said.

- **Communicate in terms team members can understand.**

    Have you ever been in a meeting and listened to a well-meaning, intelligent professional talk gibberish? Everyone has. "Gibberish" is trade talk or industry jargon — words and expressions that mean something to some specialized group somewhere but are meaningless to the general public. Hearing gibberish is a maddening experience, particularly when you really want to know and act on the information being communicated (or rather, not being communicated).

    You have three choices in those instances.

    1. Smile and nod and hope no one asks you to repeat what you've heard.

    2. Risk looking dumb by asking, "What does that word mean?"

Hearing gibberish is a maddening experience.

3. Hope someone else will look dumb and ask the questions for you.

A StaffCoach™ can't afford to put his associates in that position, especially when communicating instructions, action plans or goals.

Example

Coach (on phone):

Bernie, would you go to my office and bring a couple of things down to this meeting for me?

Bernie:

Sure, Ray, what things?

Coach:

Well, there were some year-end budget materials I've been working with. They are stacked on the far right-hand corner of my desk.

Bernie:

I think I see the pile from here.

Coach:

Good. What I need immediately from that stack are two files: the income statement and the balance sheet. The rest can wait. But everyone is waiting for those things down here.

Bernie:

No problem. Except, um …

Coach:

Yeah?

Bernie:

What do these things look like exactly?

Everybody knows what an income statement and balance sheet look like, right? Wrong. It's always a dangerous assumption to think that your team members share your experience or understand any concept critical to carrying out instructions.

3

Other clarity killers include:

— Don't be ridiculous, you know.

— I know exactly what you are thinking.

— Just use your judgment.

Communicating your expectations includes:

— Telling the individual what you want accomplished.

— Telling the individual what good performance looks like.

— Telling the individual how the performance is measured.

Example

Bernie, I need the two files on the top of the stack on the right side of the desk. They are labeled Income Statement and Balance Sheet. The files are red. Bring them down to the conference room immediately.

- **Avoid using abbreviations or nicknames even when "everyone" knows what they mean.**

    "Everybody plan on having your IRC on the TL dock ... clean and ready for old "Iron Shoulders" tomorrow morning at the latest."

    Sounds ridiculous but every organization, yours included, has pet abbreviations that save time and effort. However, for the benefit of anyone who may have forgotten, who may be new or who may confuse one abbreviation with another, the clearest instructions are always abbreviation-free! Clarifying includes adding insight about what things mean, where you can get more information, what it's all about.

- **Don't permit sight or sound competition.**

    Anyone who has ever stood on the fringes of a crowd and strained to hear a speaker above traffic noise, laughter, applause, etc., understands the importance of this rule. If your listener must resort to asking a nearby co-worker, "What did he say?" or "When did

The clearest instructions are always abbreviation-free!

93

3

Understanding is doubled or tripled when reinforced with illustrations.

he say it's due?" you're asking for trouble. If there is distracting noise in your environment, move.

- **Improve clarity by using illustrations and examples.**

Understanding is doubled or tripled when reinforced with illustrations. That's just the way the human mind works. Memory tests conducted by the 3M Corporation revealed that "a picture is worth a thousand words." Understanding and retention are enhanced when you tell, show and do.

Example

Coach:

Okay now, remember, these trucks will be overloaded if the shingles are stacked higher than (pause) ... let's see ... (looks around) ... Hank, how tall are you?

Hank:

Oh, about 5'11", I think.

Coach:

Perfect! Stack the shingles no higher than Hank and we'll be fine.

Use pictures, film strips or a CD whenever possible to clarify expectations.

Coach:

Okay, this is a bird's-eye view of the stage. Everyone understand what you're looking at? (general murmur of assent) Okay, then. Betsy, when the lights come up, you walk on the stage from Position "A" here and move to Position "B," the podium, where Cliff will have the projector controls waiting for you. Got it?

Betsy:

Is Position "A" where the stairs are?

Coach:

Right. Now, Wes, when Betsy stops at the podium, you turn your spotlight on Position "C" over here and hold it for the count of ...

The point is, every direction passed on to your associates can be clarified by communications tailored to the situation.

- **Additional communication methods might include:**

  — Role-playing: explaining by acting out a desired activity.

  — Outcome contrast: describing what not to do, usually based on past experience.

  Coach:

  So, when we finally get this display ready to ship, it should look like ... well ... Andy, remember that job we shipped for Puritan?

  Andy:

  Do I ever! (laughter)

  Coach:

  Well, it shouldn't look like that!

- **Organize before communicating.**

  In the rush of busy days, when the procedures seem obvious and the projects seem predictable, failure to organize before communicating important directions or goals is very tempting ... and very common. In spite of that, remember: Organized effort never results from disorganized input! The responsibility for project progress ... for tasks that move from start to finish smoothly, on time and without hitches ... rests squarely on the coach and his ability to outline organized activity.

  Never use shortcuts in the organizational phase of your team communications. Two ways to avoid that are the following:

  1. Write your instructions or information.

     Directions are three to four times more likely to be followed correctly when written! Why? For at least three reasons:

> *You have two chances of building a strong team without communication: slim and none.*

> *Each new day offers a manager first-rate opportunities to avoid second-rate options.*

a. The team member can reread and make notes in writing on the facts you provide.

b. Misunderstandings or inaccuracies are avoided regarding names or numbers.

c. Responsibilities and expectations are documented in advance. It may take more time and effort to put your communication in writing, but the effort will pay off in fewer errors, less time policing performance and consistency in follow-through.

2. What, Who, Why, How, Where, When, What

Whatever form your communication takes ... memo, one-on-one, team presentation, conference calls, etc. ... a formula used by many coaches to communicate informational essentials is the "3-1-3" method. The numbers represent three "W's" (what, who, why), one "H" (how) and three "W's" (where, when, what). While the order may vary, these letters represent the information elements to include in your directions.

WHAT: Explain the project, the task or goal.

WHO: Assign responsibility for follow-through.

WHY: The reasons for and benefits of the task.

HOW: What action will achieve the goal.

WHERE: Relevant project locations (conference rooms, warehouses, client offices, departments, etc.)

WHEN: The project timetable: start and finish dates.

WHAT :   The consequences of success or failure, rewards and penalties.

Here is a memo that makes obvious use of the "3-1-3" formula.

To: Will

From: Matt

Subject: Your responsibilities

As you know, production of the first 15 spring dress designs begins next Wednesday. All of us have had an opportunity for hands-on inspection of each design. None of the designs appears to be especially difficult.

WHAT

WHO

Your group will have responsibility for Designs A through E, Margaret's group for designs F through J, and Ted's group for K through O.

Naturally, the retail team needs these finished goods right on time in order to launch the new image campaign at least two weeks before the competition's drop dates.

WHY

Each of your associates should have a design-by-design specification guide. As usual, consulting those guides and checking jobs in progress are especially critical during the first four to six hours of production. If you have any questions, of course, let's talk.

HOW

The new air-conditioning unit should make the production rooms a lot more conducive to concentration. And it will be interesting to see if the vote to switch from classical to country music will improve output! Team leaders will deliver all inspected garments to rooms #1 and #2 for packaging.

WHERE

We have eight working days to meet the quotas we discussed last Friday. We all agreed that seemed like a comfortable deadline, so if we can beat it ... with error-free goods ... let's do it!

WHEN

We are still slightly ahead of the Men's Division going into the last quarter. I don't know about you, but I want that bonus! And, after all, why shouldn't the best division in the entire company have it?

WHAT

Again, call or come by with any questions or problems. My door is always open because (as you know) my office doesn't have one!

3

As mentioned, the order of your W's will vary with your situation, but the simplicity of this formula and its "catchall" power will prove to be one of your key communication allies.

Verify Understanding: How to Hear What They Think They Heard.

- **Ask questions.**

    An open, nonthreatening work environment encourages associates to ask any question anytime. The old adage, "The only dumb questions are the ones never asked," is still true and important to the ongoing growth and development of employees. Even when you are sure this freedom exists, however, the way you ask verifying questions can reveal questions your team members didn't know they had. Remember, what you think they heard may be nowhere near what was absorbed. They may not even be listening!

    "What is there that might still be a little unclear about what I've said?"

    This question, or one like it, encourages your associates to search their understanding and verbalize any doubts that may exist … especially when the coach asks it in an agreeable … even expectant … tone of voice. Simply barking the words, "Any questions?" (particularly in a group environment) is deadly. You might as well add, "Or are you too dumb to understand the first time?"

    Some managers have used the following statements to elicit employee responses.

    > *"This is pretty complicated stuff, so don't hesitate to tell me when I can make something clearer."*

    > *"I expect lots of questions about this, so just stop me if you have one."*

    > *"Let's stop now and deal with questions you have about all this. I had lots of questions myself when I first heard it."*

    Do you sense the advance acceptance in these statements?

When you are working with your average employees, clarity is vital. You want them to clearly hear that you want to help them move to that next level. You want them to buy in to doing that little bit extra.

Three statements communicate very encouraging messages.

1. *As coach, I'm not always as clear as I want to be …*

2. *I feel your questions are justified …*

3. *I've had questions like you may have right now.*

Unanswered questions are like bad checks. They will return to demand your attention … with penalties!

Be clear about why you want the associate to do more, and in what ways.

- **Hypothetical scenarios**

 Another helpful technique for flushing out misconceptions about information you've communicated is to pose hypothetical situations based on the project and procedures you have outlined.

 Example

 Coach:

 Okay, now, just to make us all feel more comfortable with what we're about to do, let's make a few assumptions. Ben, what happens if you continue answering the calls in the same manner, maintaining the time measurements, no better, no worse?

 Ben:

 I might not be eligible for a promotion to lead or get my pick of days off.

 Coach:

 Do you see that as a penalty or punishment?

 Ben:

 As you noted, I am paid to handle calls within the four minute measure. I do that and that is what my salary guarantees. But you think I can do better, adding more concern into the calls. And, that's what merit increases

> *Unanswered questions are like bad checks. They will return … with penalities!*

3

Scenarios tend to work best in a group setting.

and the department perks are all about.

Coach:

Exactly!

Ben:

I just don't see how to add more into four minutes.

Coach:

No problem, let's talk about some ways right now.

Hypothetical scenarios can be fun and enlightening, depending on the situation. A word of caution, however: Such scenarios can also sound childish or insulting to highly professional mentalities. You must make that call. In any case, scenario development is nearly always best in a group setting where individuals can interact and not feel as if they are being graded by their responses or put on the "hot seat."

• **Reports on progress**

A popular method to verify understanding of your directions is written or verbal project progress reports. These can be as simple and informal as daily or weekly coffee meetings where you casually discuss job flow. Or they can be as regimented as submitting forms at specific project points or job phases. Monday notes is one way to follow the actions of your people. Each Monday morning, employees can e-mail or give you a short, concise list of accomplishments from the previous week. A report might use the kind of outline on the following page:

Reports on Progress

WHERE WE'VE BEEN

The successes _____

The problems/setbacks _____

Questions and solutions _____

WHERE WE ARE

The successes _____

The problems/setbacks _____

Questions and solutions _____

WHERE WE'RE GOING

The successes _____

The problems/setbacks _____

Questions and solutions _____

Whether written or oral, reports should update the coach on what is going right, what isn't, what might not go right, and what uncertainties or problem-solving tactics involve the team.

Your report outline (if you choose to use one) may be quite different from this one, but a standardized structure for reporting progress can assure everyone that nothing is falling through the cracks.

• **Listen to the feedback generated by your verification efforts.**

Use the techniques important in hearing "the message behind the message" to hear both what they say and what they don't say. Watch the eyes, the face, the head position, the full-body angle. The tone of associates' responses to your questions as well as facial expressions, gestures and

"Genius begins great works; labor finishes them."

— Joubert

postures can send signals that verify or contradict their oral messages. Really effective coaches unconsciously follow the nonverbal clues that employees are with them, that they "get it," that there is agreement. Likewise, when employees say, "Sure, no problem," connected coaches do not end the conversation, but begin a series of probes to ensure understanding, agreement or further discussion.

Example

Coach:

Well, Leslie, I guess that's about it. Are you clear on everything ... any questions at all?

Leslie (furrowed brow):

Not a thing.

Coach:

Uh-huh. It's a lot to take in on such short notice. You're okay with me asking you to focus harder on the accounts and the timing?

Leslie (eyes downcast, arms folded):

It's all perfectly clear.

Coach:

I guess I'm sensing there may be something troubling you about this conversation that I may be making hard for you to share. I think it's important that we open up to each other at this stage, Leslie.

Leslie (chin lifted, eye contact from nose down, tone of resentment):

It's nothing really. I'll admit I do think you are being a little unfair. I am doing my job.

Coach:

That's perfectly true. You are doing that — just that. And, as you continue doing as well as you do, you keep raising the stakes. You are good, Leslie, really good.

3

Leslie (brightening, straightening in chair):

So this isn't about me not doing something?

Coach:

Right. It's about you working at your potential and getting the recognition you deserve. You are a huge asset for the team and I want to keep you.

Leslie (solid eye contact, leaning forward eagerly):

Well, this is clear, Gil. I've got a good handle on it. So what you want to talk about is me really contributing.

Example Analysis

Look back at Leslie's spoken responses before Gil said he was getting mixed messages. The messages are positive, but Leslie's expression, tone and posture are negative.

Being sensitive to responses and hearing more than words as you attempt to verify understanding is a learned skill. Granted, some people seem more adept, but coaching is a set of behaviors that can be practiced, learned and mastered.

Probe for the reasons behind contradictory messages. They signal underlying problems that could sabotage communication and project success. For effective probing, think open-ended listening, stating a feeling or a summary, and then becoming silent to allow the other to talk.

> *So, you are saying there are no problems.*
>
> *You feel this is unfair.*
>
> *I sense you have something else on your mind.*

> *Ideas work best when you do.*

3

Coach's Role in Affirming Associates

Affirming is a key coaching behavior. It impacts trust and trusting makes the affirmations more believable. Consider what draws you to another person: having your flaws and weaknesses pointed out or having your self-esteem enhanced? Affirming makes people listen to you and makes them want to listen to you.

There was an old leadership trick called the sandwich technique in which managers were taught to sandwich the criticism, or negative, between two positives.

> *"You handle that customer well. You were a little rushed with her; next time slow down your explanation. You really are an asset for us when it comes to handling irate people. Nice job."*

There are conflicting thoughts on this technique. For many, the affirmations to soften the criticism appear contrived. Others feel that people open up to critiques or suggestions when they know you see their worth. Think about the times your employees interrupted you with, "Wait, you don't understand, I tried ... ." When trust is established and/or you have affirmed good behaviors, people can hear your coaching suggestions for improvement.

Like rewarding employees, affirming or complimenting them on effort and attitude is an excellent motivator for continued performance. It energizes. No team member works well for long without a compliment. Susette Elgin discussed the art of verbal self-defense in her book of that title. She taught that to cause behavior, you recognized or affirmed it; to sustain behavior, you irregularly acknowledged it; and to cease a behavior, you ignored it. The attitude of some managers, "If you don't hear from me, just assume everything is fine," equates to ignoring and will not get desired results. Mark Twain said, "One good compliment can sustain me for a year." It's the same with your employees; go beyond "sustain" and encourage them to greatness.

Being comfortable with affirming others' behavior is tied to attitude on your part. Coaches with negative or poor attitudes tend to have trouble affirming others. It's often said that you can't give what you don't have inside you.

A hard concept for many coaches to realize is exactly what they must impart to their people: You choose your attitude. Fact:

> *No team member works well for long without a compliment.*

3

Thoughts cause feelings and feelings cause behavior. There are only two options here.

1. **Keep thinking those negative thoughts.**

   Wake up in the morning or drive to work thinking, "another day, what problems now, I can't believe these people," letting the thoughts roll over and over in your mind. It pulls you down. Negative thoughts = negative attitudes. Allow this thought process to continue and everything is colored by the negative lens through which your mind views the day. The drive to work is chaos. It seems that all you encounter at work is bad news. Even the good news isn't as good as it could be. Unless something happens to jar you out of this negative mindset (i.e., you win the Publisher's Clearinghouse Sweepstakes), your day will end no better than it started — and the next morning it will pick up where it left off! Worse, it spills over to the team. An affirmation would sound more like a grudging comment.

   Cherie Carter-Scott, author and coach, labeled "negaholism" a constant state of negativity. One reason for this ailment is habit, simply allowing yourself to float into negativity. Negative attitude and improved performance just don't equate.

2. **Think of the things you look forward to about your day.**

   A second choice is to focus on the positives. This rarely happens automatically — at first. Positive thoughts have to be a conscious choice.

   This is a skill important to have and to teach your people. Some ideas to help you include the following:

   - Make a list of all the things you like about your work. It may start slowly but one or two positives will multiply as you ponder. The list can act as your 80–20 guide. Keep your attention on the 80 percent of the job that you find positive.

   - Psycho-cybernetics, taught by author Bobbe Sommer, suggests a technique called cancel, cancel. Whenever

> *Worry is interest paid on trouble before it is due.*

> *Thoughts cause feelings and feelings cause behavior.*

the negative thought comes to mind, repeat out loud: cancel cancel.

- A third technique is to deny access. You can take control of your attitude by simply blocking out the negative. When the negative thought starts coming into your consciousness, tell yourself you won't take that thought or that person with you, into the office, or into your home at night.

- Scott Peck wrote about "Thirty Golden Minutes." He noted that your mind is most susceptible during the four to 10 minutes before falling asleep and the 16 to 20 minutes when awaking. Consciously put in affirmations and positives. Repeat them, and allow your attitude to take on those thoughts.

Teach your people how to change their attitudes and change their minds. This can be one of the most powerful influences you have on your people's performances. With a positive mindset, they can take over their own responsibility to grow their skills and take their actions to higher levels.

An excellent action to connect this important technique — your own attitude and that of your people — is to list the job strengths and positive character traits of one team member per day. This will strengthen your overall attitude toward him as well as give you the means to honestly affirm him on a regular basis.

An example of this is shown on the following form. It illustrates what you could note about Robert. Read what was written, then consider one of your associates. Who is an employee who has been on your mind? Write down four compliments that you can honestly give that employee. Our brains tend to focus on negative memories rather than on the potential for new tomorrows. If you were told to write down four reasons why that same person is a problem employee, it would probably be much easier.

3

Team Booster Forms

Team Member: _Robert_

Attribute	Compliment	Date Done
Never misses work.	If everyone had your attendance record, we'd probably always be ahead of schedule.	Mon. 2/4
Quiet. Doesn't disturb others by talking loudly.	We all need to help each other concentrate on the job by keeping our voices down ... like Robert.	
Desk is always neat.	It's nice to know there's an orderly desk I can show when clients drop in.	
Doesn't take long.	Thanks for being trustworthy about lunch hours.	

Team Booster Forms

Team Member: _____

Attribute	Compliment	Date Done

Exercise Analysis

Notice in the example that none of these positive attributes is exceptionally noteworthy. There may be no mention of job achievements or professional skills. Many of the qualities you find to compliment in your own team members may fall into similar categories. But track the process for a few months and you'll begin to find new positive things to say as your team responds to your affirmation! As with any skill, practice, and remember what Vince Lombardi cautioned, "Practice doesn't make perfect, perfect practice makes perfect." Affirming your people is perfect practice for causing great results. When you have trust and clear expectations of roles, you can never affirm and compliment too much. Everything you recognize will be received as truthful and focused.

The Coach's Role in Motivating and Inspiring

A fourth accountability in the coaching process is helping your people become and stay energized. It means pumping up your people from the outside until they gradually begin energizing themselves from the inside. Coaching does have cheerleading in it. When you are involved with your people, you earn their trust by being real, by respecting their points of view, by keeping the lines of communication clear, and by affirming their efforts to be the best they can be. This is motivation, and this is where their inspiration to greater performance can come from. It isn't what you do to them, it's what you do around them that lets them do it to themselves.

In short, motivation and inspiration are the logical outgrowths of everything you have read in this chapter up to this point. Logical, but not automatic. As coach, you still provide the vision — a focus and direction. While a manager creates the team's vision, the coach gets personal. Your inspiration is for people to feel about their vision, their goals, the direction they are taking. That is why StaffCoaching™ is not about what you do, but about what they do. You provide the challenge to look beyond the tasks at hand to new horizons.

For instance, realizing that money is not always the best performance motivator, listen carefully and observe your people to know what they consider worthy and important. Every serious study of team behavior over the last 30 years shows that numerous short-term and long-term career incentives are more important than income increases when it comes to energizing employee performance, morale and loyalty.

Demonstrating that you care for employees as unique individuals inspires today's workforce.

Based on those studies, the following exercise is designed to help you find motivators of special relevance to your own people. Remember: Think of answers you believe would be especially significant as motivators in your own special team environment.

1. Shared Goals

In the blanks on the left, list three goals you and your associates would consider desirable ... unanimously. Product quality might be a common goal. Manageable deadlines might be another. What others would be uniquely true for you and the people on your team? In the blanks at the right, write one step that could be taken to achieve each goal. A step for product quality might be to pay more attention to the specs or have a team member check another's work.

Unanimous Goal   **Step to Achieve**

- _____   _____
- _____   _____
- _____   _____

2. Self-Esteem

List three ways you might increase the self-esteem of your associates, individually. Be specific and realistic. Don't say, "Compliment them more often." Instead say, "Compliment Patrick on his performance twice a week starting at lunch next Tuesday." What other ways can you help maintain the self-esteem of the people on your team?

- _____
- _____
- _____

3

3. Good Communication

In the blanks at the left, list three ways you can improve communication between team members. Maybe a Friday afternoon "Coffee & Recap" meeting would help air out any lingering problems or resentments. How about an employee-produced newsletter? Some teams have eliminated killer comments by having a jar in their manager's office. Anytime someone says a putdown or killer comment, and another associate calls it, the instigator puts in a quarter. Proceeds pay for a special team celebration. Use your imagination — and solicit ideas from the entire team. In the blanks at the right, write one step that could be taken to achieve each goal.

Communication Improvement   **Step to Achieve**

- _____   _____

- _____   _____

- _____   _____

4. Growth Opportunity

In the blanks at the left, list three ways to empower your associates. Are there functions performed by you or a supervisor that the team could do? Are there procedures that might be improved from within the team rather than imposed from outside? For instance, do you have a problem-solving committee among your team members to handle selected difficulties? Is there an idea development committee? Have you considered asking team members to write their own job descriptions? How might your team members be encouraged to take ownership in company plans and policies — and grow as individuals — through new responsibilities? In the blanks at the right, write one step that could be taken to achieve each goal.

Empowerment Opportunity   **Step to Achieve**

- _____   _____

- _____   _____

- _____   _____

5. Trust and Respect

In the blanks at the left, identify three ways to build mutual trust and respect between you and your team members. Do you spend individual time with each member weekly (not just to correct them)? What could you do that would show your commitment to the team's best interests without sacrificing organizational standards or goals? Have you ever ordered in pizza and invited team members to a luncheon brainstorm session? Do you have a team picnic? Dinner? Night out at the ball game? What could you do to demonstrate your belief that you have the best group of people any manager could ask for? In the blanks at the right, write one step that could be taken to achieve each goal.

Trust Builder   **Step to Achieve**

- _____   _____

- _____   _____

- _____   _____

Exercise Analysis

The five elements of the exercise are the keys for achieving results. You encourage greater performance from your okay employees by sharing goals, building self-esteem, communicating, appreciating. It is a self-perpetuating cycle with each element supporting another. With this exercise you also just compiled a list of nonmoney motivators that can bolster morale, improve performance and heighten commitment at least as much as a salary increase. Put them to work today!

Some Cautions for the Coach

There are pitfalls to coaching. They serve as a summary for what to do to cause your people to produce results. Avoiding the pitfalls is all about doing what excellent coaches do.

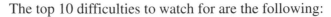

3

The top 10 difficulties to watch for are the following:

1. You don't determine what is worthy performance.

2. You aren't clear about what you expect.

3. You don't have enough information about your people.

4. You are inflexible about how to perform.

5. You lose it when your employee is negative toward your coaching.

6. You become defensive.

7. You don't get feedback or suggestions or solutions from your people.

8. You don't listen to what your people are saying.

9. You don't hold individuals accountable for their performance measures.

10. You fail to reinforce improved performance.

Steps for Effective Coaching Interactions

Whenever you coach your people, your approach will depend on the situation and what you are attempting. The following steps give you a general guideline for interacting with your people. Using it will keep you out of the 10 pitfalls just listed.

1. Put the employee at ease by being warm, friendly and open.

2. Clearly and immediately define what you want to discuss.

3. Explain why you are concerned about the specific area of performance even though the employee is meeting standards.

4. Describe what the employee can do to use more of his potential.

5. Acknowledge and listen to the employee's feelings.

6. Ask how the employee thinks he can move his performance to the next level.

7. Ask open-ended questions to encourage the employee to determine his own solutions.

8. Let the employee know that you respect his ability to get results.

9. Build on any ideas your employee has and continue to pull from him.

10. Agree upon specific actions he can take and you can do.

11. Schedule another meeting to discuss what has occurred from now to then.

12. Commit to provide feedback, encouragement and attention to the employee.

The steps for a coaching session essentially focus on communication, honoring your associate and establishing a continuous relationship of support.

Common Activities for the Coach

Activities that are included in this approach of the StaffCoach™ Model vary depending upon your employee. Anything you do, however, is for the purpose of encouraging more than average performance. Avoiding the pitfalls and working within the steps give you a big range. Things that a coach commonly does include the following:

- Listening to the employee talk about himself, his job, his issues.

- Watching the employee interact with others.

- Showing the employee what others do that surpass performance.

- Asking about reasons for doing some of the tasks as he does.

- Taping the employee and listening together to how he does his job.

- Videotaping the employee and watching together how he does his job.

- Reviewing why enough isn't enough.

- Demonstrating where the employee surpassed his own performance.

- Underscoring the employee's successes.

- Persuading the employee to take on more.

Each action taken by the coach implies follow-up. You don't call attention to something and walk away. Neither do you set up something and walk away. This is beyond Tom Peters' MBWA. With any action you take, your goal is clear: Motivate your employee to do more. Hence, the approach is continuous: You tell, show, demonstrate, praise, explain, tell, praise, have him tell, praise — on and on, in and out — as you shape his performance.

What to Expect When You're Doing It Right

As an effective coach, you will begin to immediately experience very specific, very real results. People respond to caring and recognition. You will motivate and energize yourself by the results you see in your people. When associates start growing and changing and accepting responsibility for their own performances, you know you are contributing.

Remember: Use your coaching role for people who are performing above their job standards. In the coaching role, your primary goals are to initiate or affirm a relationship that builds trust; clarifies and verifies your communications; supports, motivates and inspires. These are some of the results you can expect to see when you are effectively performing that role.

1. Clarification of performance expectations

2. Changes in point of view

3. Increased self-sufficiency/autonomy

4. Insight into behavior and feelings

5. Acceptance of difficult tasks

Clarification of Performance Expectations

When you properly perform the coaching role, both you and your team members have a clearer understanding of what performance is expected. Because you talk with your people, you have a clearer picture of what each can do. And they get a clearer picture of what you expect. Help people see that, while you are paying them for performance, it is potential that you want. Quite often, this increased communication inspires both of you to greater achievement.

Changes in Point of View

Because you are involved, respecting team members' opinions and affirming their skills and goals, you will learn more about other people's points of view. And because you are encouraging and inspiring others, you will affect their points of view — helping them catch a new and broader perspective and professional vision. It is too easy to be myopic in any given job.

Increased Self-Sufficiency/Autonomy

An important outcome of effective coaching is the increase in the self-sufficiency and autonomy of team members. The coaching role should help give team members a freeing, new identity … a sense of responsibility for their own performance growth. It imparts confidence. It can minimize a tendency for the status quo. It allows team members to rechannel "ego energy" into collective goals. Once team members are secure about how you view them … and how they can perform … they are willing and receptive to use more of their potential. They can act to energize teammates who may not be as self-sufficient.

> *Being coached should help give team members a sense of importance.*

Insight Into Behavior and Feelings

The more you coach, the more you learn about your people, and the more you learn about yourself. You grow your own insights into human behavior and emotions. This increased sensitivity to the contextual nature of results adds to your power in influencing behaviors.

3

The managerial style of the new millennium is one of responsiveness and empathy. This is in part due to the demands of the new workforce and in part due to the number of women in management equaling their male counterparts. Regardless of the origin of the emphasis, the impact is real. Recognize how someone feels and you deal with the complete person.

Break Old Habits of Responding

Developing coaching skills requires you to change your mind as well as your people's minds. Telling and doing behaviors must switch to facilitating and observing ones. It's more important to discuss what your people can do than what they're doing.

Like any behavior, one challenge to you is habit. Coaches often respond to people in a knee-jerk fashion, reacting as managers.

A Three-Step Process to Monitor the "Knee-jerk" Response Tendency

When someone does or says something that bothers you, instead of blowing up, stop and take a deep breath. Then ask yourself three questions:

1. **"What part of this problem is the employee's and what part may be mine?"**

   For instance, have you ever been given "great" tickets to a sporting or an arts event, only to discover that you are much farther from the action than you imagined? You find yourself sitting there seething inwardly about the injustice of it all … even when the seats are free!

   The same situation can occur in the work environment when team members' attitudes or actions conflict with your expectations. Someone's choice of clothing may be inappropriate for a client presentation. Someone's phone manner may seem at times grating or insensitive. Maybe those observations are accurate and need to be addressed, rather than waiting until there is a performance problem. But first examine yourself — avoid a knee-jerk response! You may find that the difficulty lies in your negative expectations, not in the actual behavior.

2. **"What is the specific feeling that I'm choosing to feel because of this action?"**

    Note the key word, "choosing." You have the ability to reject or accept feelings. As a coach, you have the responsibility to do that!

3. **"What is the root reason for my feelings?"**

    What lies at the core of your anger, frustration, disappointment or bitterness? Does it really bear on this specific action or does it have its roots in something totally unrelated?

    None of us approaches any experience totally free of previous experiences. Each has a history he brings to a task. Both positive and negative experiences have value, and we learn from bad as well as good. But if we're not careful, we can also allow experiences from the past to hinder or prevent positive responses in the present.

    The truth is, a bad haircut really can prompt you to respond more negatively to people and events than you would have normally. An unexplained dent in your new car can give you an excuse to sound curt to a client on the phone. But, knowing that, you must evaluate your responses — otherwise, your team members will begin to feel like children waiting for mom's or dad's mood to improve before approaching either of them with something important.

    Have you ever been upset and not really known why? Someone asks, "What's wrong?" and you say, "I don't know." And you really don't. You're not in control. When you ask yourself the three questions listed above, you're getting yourself under control so you can talk to people as an adult and not as an irate parent trying to punish a child for doing something wrong. Act … don't react.

Act … don't react!

Acceptance of Difficult Tasks

There's one more outcome you can expect if you have effectively assumed the role of coach. Your team members will accept increasingly difficult tasks. This is a natural result of team

members having a clearer understanding of your expectations —
as well as the confidence to work more independently. The
coaching role is to encourage that growth. Challenge your people.
Let them know that you have confidence in them. Let them know
that you think they are "unlimited resources." Let them know that
you think they can do and be whatever they choose — and show
them how.

Case Study

Neil Evans joined the staff of a private southern college as
director of food services just three weeks after the former director
died suddenly in an automobile accident. When the associate
director learned that he would not be offered the vacated post, he
resigned immediately. So Neil took over a 37-person team with
only four days to review records, accounts, menus and personnel
files … as well as inspect the campus food-service complex.

His past experience directing food services for the dormitories
at a state university helped his orientation process greatly, but he
admitted to the college president that he would be "feeling his
way" through some areas without the detailed input of the two
previous staff leaders.

His first act as director was to call a Saturday morning
meeting of the entire food-service staff, before any of the food
facilities were active. He had five items to discuss.

1. Introduce himself.

2. Assure everyone that someone was at the helm.

3. Deal with rumors surrounding the associate
   director's resignation.

4. Discuss his immediate goals.

5. Answer any questions team members might have.

After he covered his first three points, Neil passed out a list of
his short-term goals. He also placed them on an overhead projector
while he spoke. His goals were the following:

1. Meet with every employee in the next two weeks to discuss:

   a. The strengths and weaknesses of the school's food-service program from each employee's point of view.

   b. The special concerns and dreams of each employee.

   c. Ideas for growth: the employee's as well as the program's.

2. Thoroughly familiarize himself with working environments in all five food-service outlets: the Student Union Cafeteria, the alum and faculty "Regency Restaurant" (also located in the Union), The Snack Shop and the two dormitory cafeterias — and to hold team meetings with the complete staffs of each.

3. Establish an administrative committee that would function in the vacated role of associate director. The committee would be composed of the five current staff managers, plus three team-elected members. The duties of the committee were to be defined in upcoming brainstorm sessions.

The time Neil had anticipated for the question session proved too short. Many members had questions. It was apparent that loyalties existed to the associate who resigned — as well as much anger at the president over treatment and salary issues. Neil noted the essence of each remark or complaint on overheads for all to see. By the time the session was over, he had 11 note-packed overhead transparencies!

Neil concluded the meeting by promising to transcribe each remark, to study each and report his conclusions to everyone within one month.

The days ahead were busy ones for Neil. He asked for and was given an office in the Student Union building instead of the office of the past director, which was located across from the president's office in the Administrative Building. He met daily with the five managers of each food-service outlet to discuss current operations and to brainstorm methods to improve service and profitability. Once the three newly elected committee members had joined these meetings, an additional daily meeting was added to study personnel policies and practices.

C A S E S T U D Y

He met daily with at least two members of the food-service team, one during breakfast and the other over lunch, getting to know more about each, and generally covering the three areas he had outlined for them in his introductory meeting.

In addition to his daily meetings, Neil worked half-days for one week in each of the college's food-service facilities. He did everything from waiting tables and cooking to cleaning up, planning menus and operating cash registers.

In a little over four weeks, Neil called another early morning team meeting. He opened that meeting by welcoming the "Food Brood." He confessed that he was a few days late regarding his promise to report on questions and remarks collected from the introductory meeting. At that point, he turned over the meeting to the Food Service Administrative Committee. The committee passed out folders titled, *"Where We Are and Where We're Going ... Together!"* They gave a one-hour presentation covering:

1. The new committee-created mission statement.

2. Ten new employee policies and benefits based on employee remarks in the introductory meeting.

3. A new "profit-sharing" bonus plan tied to each facility team's ability to create and implement new cost-saving, revenue-generating measures.

Employees were encouraged to complete and return an "Impressions and Evaluations" form included in each folder to their team leaders in one week.

Then the meeting was opened for questions. Committee members were able to answer the surprisingly few questions that were asked without input from Neil. When it was apparent that there were no more questions, Neil stood to conclude the meeting.

He began by requesting a round of applause for the eight-member administrative committee. It was their efforts, he assured the group, that made the many positive new steps a reality. Then he expressed his gratitude to the president, who had reviewed the entire plan just presented and had approved it wholeheartedly. He then thanked the entire group for the fun of working alongside them, for allowing him to get to know them, and for the loyalty and commitment he saw in each person.

He concluded by telling the group that in only a short time every member had made him feel like "family," and that he was already as proud as the past director undoubtedly was to be associated with them.

Case Analysis

Neil Evans demonstrated real coaching strengths in the scenario you just read. He took over a team that was functioning well and he maintained and surpassed performance measures. He worked for buy-in, and took care not to allow negativity or lack of drive to creep in. You get the feeling that his food-service team is going to benefit greatly from his leadership.

Consider some specifics that can give you deeper insights into the scenario — and into your own team/coach relationship.

1. What did the associate director's resignation tell you about the leadership style prior to Neil's arrival?
   What message might the resignation have sent to the 37-member staff?

2. In his two total-team meetings, do you think Neil communicated clearly? How?

3. Did he provide opportunities to verify employee understanding? How?

4. Was Neil's choice of offices significant to you? Good or bad? Why?

C A S E   S T U D Y

3

3

5. Was Neil's decision to have an administrative committee rather than an associate director a wise one? Why?

6. If you were a member of Neil's 37-person team, would you trust his motives in waiting tables, washing dishes, etc., or would you feel he was just "slumming"? Why or why not?

7. What other "involvement" steps did Neil take in his coaching role?

8. Would the food-service team be motivated and inspired by the plans unveiled by the committee? Why or why not?

9. Do you think Neil did anything to help eliminate resentment expressed toward the president in the first team meeting? Explain.

10. Do you think his concluding remarks about "family" were appropriate? Explain.

You may be thinking that it is much easier to write or talk about coaching than it is to do it! But the encouraging fact is that real-life situations ... much more chaotic and potentially disastrous than Neil's case study ... have been and are being handled capably by StaffCoaching™ principles.

Summary

The coaching approach in the StaffCoach™ Model is for average performers. With this role you support and affirm, motivate and encourage, inspire and get buy-in. A coach requires trust and that comes about through involvement, communication and clarity of goals.

People are more willing to enter into a symbiotic relationship with you when they know you believe in them, will stand by them, and are open to their thoughts and feelings. Communication, both in setting goals and in listening to feedback, is instrumental in taking people from where they are to where they can be.

There are pitfalls, and there are steps to serve as a guide. Process is one word that summarizes the entire coach role. It isn't an instance-by-instance activity. One interaction builds on another. Connection and relationship are the bridges that let you get across to your people that they are the most important asset of the organization, that you are successful because of and through them, and your job is to do anything possible to help them reach optimum performance.

The coaching role is a continuous part of the manager and employee relationship. As in the story about the turtle and the hare, it is the slow and steady, the constant and always confident progress toward the goal that wins the race. You can coach all types of fancy moves and clever "flavor of the month" tactics, but it all comes down to involvement and belief in your people, to trusting that they can always do better. There's the next game, the next project, and, of course, tomorrow.

3

?
___

Chapter Quiz

1. What employees are the best candidates for the coaching role? Who would fit that description on your team?

2. What four key attributes characterize the coaching role?

3. Name four ways to establish coach/team member trust. Which are you weakest in?

4. What method of verifying your communication to the team appeals most to you? Which one haven't you tried?

5. Which method of affirming your team members would work best in your environment?

6. Name three nonmoney motivators from this chapter that you currently use.

CHAPTER 4

The Mentoring Role: Instruction by Example

The mentoring role is reserved for managing those people whose performance is above average. Mentor your stars, individuals who are mature, experienced and wise in the business. While the catchwords for coaching are "inspire" and "motivate," the catchwords for mentoring are "instruct" and "guide." When you mentor, it's your job to teach new skills and explain different outlooks. Typically, that's how the star performers will align their career aspirations and goals with your organization. Mentoring is all about giving people broader outlooks, more things to consider. It is for career planning, succession planning and retention.

People want to be around people who are exceptional. Tom Peters noted that two real motivators were being part of a winning team and being a winner. While mentoring is often given lip service in business, it is a reality in organizations with winners and winning teams. While coaching identifies potential and deals with problems, mentoring lets employees soak up character, judgment and approach. It is the opportunity for them to apprise situations and cultivate their own ways.

You might think of a coach as walking behind, prompting, and a counselor as being in front, pulling. Think of a mentor as a person who walks alongside the associate. In the mentoring role, you "come alongside" the people on your team. You work with them side by side, giving instruction —

> *Like it or not, you are the example.*

125

and not just verbal instruction. It's "hands-on" instruction. It's doing the task together. You lead by example, demonstrating additional ways for success. Mentors dig deeper, are more involved in the whole person.

This approach is separate from coaching and counseling. One reason is that every team follows what its coach "models." A coach or a counselor is change-oriented while a mentor is growth-oriented; the orientation here moves from certain behaviors or skills to overall job and life performance. You mentor by advice, by your wisdom. You mentor through stories of what others have done in situations similar to the associate's. You mentor by leading her to other mentors, other situations to learn from, other resources from which to gain insights. Certainly as a mentor, your values and walking your talk are important. A mentor doesn't, however, have to be the top performer herself; she has to be top performing.

Besides instructing and leading by example and wisdom, your other task as a mentor is to develop new abilities and interests in the people you work with. You'll help people develop new skills and outlooks … help them do things they never knew they could do. You'll teach people how to understand and use potential to their fullest.

There are many opportunities for mentoring.

- When an associate receives a promotion or new responsibilities

- After a success

- When the associate wants more than successes or promotions

- When things occur which challenge her dreams or course of action

Whenever you take an employee under your wing, the employee gets a head start for advancement and will acquire more know-how about the work, the organization and the tricks of the trade. Everything from office politics to the ins and outs of networking will make sense. This unique relationship, different from the other approaches in the StaffCoach™ Model, benefits both you and your people.

A Process With Productive Purpose

The mentoring process requires a commitment of time and a plan. It's a process of development ... not a practice of shooting from the hip. No leader arrives at work Monday morning and announces, "I'm going to mentor you; let's go." Instead, each mentor builds a specific approach. The successful plan builds on three components.

1. Mutual trust and commitment

2. Patient leadership

3. Emotional maturity

Mutual Trust and Commitment

Mutual trust and commitment come from spending time together. The more time you spend teaching someone, the more commitment you have to that person and that person has to you. Trust is one of the universals that supersedes all the aspects of coaching. The mentor is a confidante and the employee entrusts her with her dreams and fears.

Mentoring can involve huge blocks of time. Commitment implies that the mentor is accessible when the employee needs to talk, complain or voice concerns. Mentoring often occurs at the end of a day or into the evening — on your time. You can see the slight difference in this approach versus coaching. Some managers wrongly believe that their intentions to mentor are 90 percent of the battle, and that the other 10 percent involves the actual work. Two dangers exist in harboring this illusion.

1. When the truth hits home that the formula is actually reversed — 10 percent intention and 90 percent hands-on, day-to-day effort, some managers become so discouraged that they never really get started. Which leads to the second danger ...

2.   The team member may perceive that she is not worth special attention and grows to distrust not only your motives, but eventually her value and ability. Mentoring isn't giving advice and then being done.

Mentoring is hard work and it takes time. In the '60s and '70s, it was difficult for women to find mentors. Other women who had achieved places of stature in their organizations either didn't feel they had the time to support other women (especially when there was no one for them) or they were suspicious. "If I help her, she'll take my job." This attitude changed as more women managers entered higher levels and as the mentoring role became honored within organizations. Many corporations — GE, Motorola — and the federal government have established formal programs for mentoring. As an approach for leadership and a successful role in the manager's repertoire, it works.

Patient Leadership

Patience is extremely important in the mentoring process. Once you've established the commitment and trust, you maintain it through patience. As the relationship progresses, the trust and comfort level build. By using some of the principles of coaching, setting goals, and being clear on expectations, the process will evolve strongly. But, as with any exercise in human development, there are short-term and long-term gains. Coaching will produce short to medium results; mentoring is a long-haul, results-getting process. Patience adds value in the following three basic areas:

1.   **Employee attentiveness**

The things you think are important about certain concepts and procedures may not seem all that important to your associate.

Example

Coach:

The key to this phase of the job, Rhonda, is watching this set of figures here. They will tell you instantly if this product is safe to send on ahead. Do you understand that?

"Why can't we have patience and expect good things to take time?"

— John Wooden

Rhonda:

Sure. Okay, let's talk about how to develop more skill in negotiating.

Coach:

Negotiating? Well, absolutely. However, these numbers are what the CEO is watching. Whether we think they are vital or not is a different issue. If you are going to make an impact with that group, know the numbers before you dazzle them with negotiating skill.

Impatience would tempt anyone to say something like, "Earth to Rhonda: wake up … this process is lots more important than what you can do to dazzle." Remember, your associate's perceived response to information is related to what she thinks is important. Today's Generation Y and Generation X have little patience with the big picture or politics or sensitivities. They think that it's too bad if you don't get it. Patience is important on both parts — outlooks may be totally opposite. No one will ever mirror another's values or priorities perfectly. Don't expect it.

Naturally, if inattentiveness becomes a real problem, you will have to deal with it as a counselor. But be ready to exercise patience by giving your associate an explanation, some time and overview after overview.

2. **Employee aptitude**

Some people learn faster than others. As obvious as that may sound, it is hard to remember it in a mentoring situation. Your protégée may be way ahead of your most "difficult" explanations … finishing sentences for you … evidencing an advanced grasp of concepts it took you much longer to "own." More likely, however, she may require very precise, step-by-step explanations from you in order to effectively apply information in an actual work situation. High performers may have great competencies, but that doesn't necessarily equate with overall understanding and insights. Your two key jobs as a mentor in this area are to:

> *Some people learn faster than others.*

- Evaluate the team member's understanding with questions like, "What have I said that could be a little clearer?" or "If you were explaining this to someone else, how would you do it?"

- Encourage your associate to feel perfectly comfortable asking questions by telling her to feel that way ... and by responding maturely when the questions come.

Fast learner or not-so-fast learner, your associate can learn from your patient approach to her training needs.

3. **Pressure to attend to "business as usual"**

Finding time in your already overcrowded schedule to mentor one or more team members will take some doing. But it can be done. Thousands of successful coaches are making it happen. Many follow the simple but effective "15-5-10" formula.

- 15

  Rank your daily duties in order of importance and break out the bottom 15 percent.

- 5

  Delegate that 15 percent to selected team members, using 5 percent of the time you saved to continue directing them and reviewing their work.

- 10

  Use the remaining 10 percent for mentoring activities.

And where does patience come into play in this area? The inclination to resent or begrudge the time you spend away from "normal" job activities will grow as you progress in your mentoring projects. It's a natural tendency. You will be tempted to postpone or skip mentoring opportunities in the interest of "more important things." When that happens, remember:

- You aren't "losing" time while you mentor — you're using free time made available because you delegated duties.

- Your associate will know in a minute if you view your time with her as a time-wasting inconvenience.

The "15-5-10" Formula

4

So have patience with the mentoring process and clearly see its value in your overall job accountabilities.

Emotional Maturity

Maturity on both sides is required in a mentoring process. An effective mentor (or any other leader, for that matter) controls her emotions for the sake of effective leadership. Even when you're sick of hearing the same questions over and over again, you must remain (or appear to remain) calm and eager to help.

Always remain calm and eager to help.

Emotional control and handling anger figure into the values of effective StaffCoaches™. Mentors teach and exercise control, they aren't born calm. You can use many methods to build emotional control while guiding an associate to comprehend the bigger issues. These include:

- **See the mentoree as your child or your special project.**

  Everyone is someone's child. So when the questions seem especially irrelevant ... when your tendency to explode or give up seems impossible to push down ... think how the associate's parents would want you to react. Think how you would want a manager to respond if the associate were your child, or your brother or sister, etc. Silly? Forget age and get personal.

  Seeing the associate as your project implies that you have chosen this for your next accomplishment. Many coaches have a project each season. They take on one associate and nurture and develop her to independence and the next level of success in her life. Seeing mentoring as a project puts a timeline on it and provides markers for successes along the way. It's a technique that adds satisfaction and accomplishment.

- **Schedule mentoring sessions to end with "rewards."**

  Having something to look forward to can minimize emotional intensity. Anger is less likely to grip you when you're about to do something pleasurable. So schedule your mentoring sessions to end with lunch or quitting time, or even to take place during leisure events. Go into

4

mentoring sessions with pleasant expectations. If you think mentoring sessions will be dreary, painful experiences, identify why and consider talking to the associate about this experience. Mentoring sessions should be win-win experiences for both of you. But they can be demanding and a bit draining, as any good teacher will tell you. So anticipate and prepare for the possibility of frayed nerves.

- **Speak with a smile.**

    Emotional upheaval is usually accompanied by raised voices and "strained" facial features (frowns, etc.). Anger, fear and indignation are virtually impossible to express (for long) with a smiling face and soft, conversational tones. Moral: When emotions threaten to distort your normally mature responses, take a deep breath … consciously speak more softly … and smile! It does more than hide inner turmoil. It actually defuses it!

    In Uganda, farmers pair the young, beginner ox with an older ox. The two oxen are tied together with a special harness. The device is called a training yoke and it is configured to make sure the older ox pulls most of the burden. The older ox has the control. If the farmers don't do that, the younger ox tends to go too fast or too slow. The older ox has the control so it'll go at the right pace. The younger one must work at the same pace. The young ox learns from the experience of "walking alongside." If you've never mentored before, keep this illustration in mind in the days and years ahead. It will begin to have special relevance as you interact with associates.

> *"Soft words bring hard things to pass."*
> — Aesop

Ten Tips for Mentors

A guideline for what you can do as an effective mentor involves ten basics.

1. **Know your work.** Review the basics. Think back on the problems you've faced and know how you dealt with them. Be prepared to answer questions about every aspect of the focus of your mentoring.

2. **Know your organization.** One of your main functions is to help the associate overcome the hurdles in moving up and around office politics, policies and procedures. As someone who's been around, you can give her a sense of the inner workings without the years necessary in learning such.

3. **Get to know your associate.** Take the time to learn as much as you can about her background, her education, her skills and interests. Know her family, how she was raised, her outside interests. Observe personality traits, get accustomed to her way of writing, speaking and acting.

4. **Learn to teach.** Figure out how people think, how they process information. Know the adult methods for educating. Read about giving high-impact presentations and the secrets to powerful training.

5. **Learn to learn.** It is essential for a mentor to constantly take in information — not only the latest techniques in your own field, but developments in your industry, in the business community and in parallel fields. Know how to move both laterally and in a hop-scotch pattern that mimics current career progression.

6. **Be patient.** Understand human nature and develop compassion toward and awareness of the different levels and ways in which people learn. Be especially patient with the different generations. The workers today — the veterans, the baby boomers, Generation X and Generation Y — have very different points of view. They may challenge you, appear rude and be curt in their demands.

7. **Be tactful.** Kind, courteous and gentle also fit. And all are a part of being firm. You must let the associate know that you expect the optimum, the very best.

8. **Take risks.** Give your associate assignments that challenge her. Let her know that she won't succeed in all the assignments, but that the best way to grow is by taking the tough job. Tell her that you will back her.

4

9. **Celebrate successes.** Let your associate know that you are proud of her accomplishments and the progress she makes. Celebrate significant milestones. Make this a fun and exciting collaboration.

10. **Encourage your associate to be a mentor.** This is part of the full-cycle process that is at the heart of all the skills and elements of coaching. Continue what you are doing through your associate.

The Six Ways People Think

One of the main reasons to mentor someone is to instruct or guide her. For that reason, the impact of your mentoring will depend on how well you are able to teach. And how well you teach depends on how well you understand how adults learn. If every adult learned exactly the same way, your job might not be especially challenging. But the truth is that everyone learns differently!

The learning process depends on how people accept or receive knowledge. Understanding the six basic ways people think and appreciating that people learn differently will enable you to connect with them. A thinking style is no better or worse than another. Like communication and personality styles, a thinking style sometimes has an appropriateness in one place or another. When you understand how your associate thinks, and how she receives information, you can tailor your explanations to that style. Result: instant understanding. Your message gets through; there is connection. StaffCoaching™ suspends judgment. People are there for you to support and guide. Know the way your associate thinks, what's important to her and how she takes in your comments, and you can zero in on persuasion and buy-in.

The six ways people think and process information follow:

1. Authority driven
2. Deductive
3. Sensory
4. Emotional
5. Intuitive
6. Scientific

Authority-driven Thinkers

Some people best accept and process knowledge by taking specific direction from authority. If you mentor these people, all you usually have to do is tell them to do something. You're the boss. They'll do it. Many coaches prefer this kind of employee. Such a person rarely talks back or questions orders. Those can be commendable characteristics, but remember also that problems can arise in dealing with people who respond to authority with knee-jerk obedience. They may do whatever you tell them to do, but sometimes they don't do anything unless you tell them.

Many people think this way because they were taught early on by authority figures and made to obey, not question. One challenge for you is to encourage and develop independent thinking. As a mentor, you can capitalize on the strengths of this style while ridding it of much weakness. Your task is to recognize where the line of motivation exists within each authority-driven team member, and help her recognize it, too.

Example

Coach:

Jan, this newsletter headline is the old one. Didn't you substitute a new emergency headline like we discussed?

Jan:

I rushed it to the editorial department like you said. I even did it on my lunch hour. But you didn't tell me what to change — I thought you wanted this one.

Coach:

The newsletter was already on the press. That headline had to be added before the run started! Jan, you can write headlines.

Jan:

Gee, that's a creative job, yours, and I didn't want to offend you.

Coach:

I don't have to okay everything for you. You are good. But the good news is the press broke down. They only ran off a

Authority-driven thinkers may not do anything unless you tell them.

4

135

few copies like this one. So write a new headline now and get it in to editorial.

Jan:

You bet!

Coach:

And, Jan ... what are you going to do with it this time?

Jan:

I'll make sure the press people know we're altering the plates, and then I'll go straight to typesetting.

Coach:

Great thinking. Go for it!

Deductive Thinkers

Another way people accept or process facts is through deductive reasoning. When you mentor people whose minds work this way, you must make things logical. These people prefer linear, analytical explanations — point A to point B. You have to go into detail ... sometimes almost defending your own thought processes. These people have to understand each step. When you stop and say, "Okay, now you go ahead and do it," they'll probably say, "Can you run through that one more time, please?" If you're a Type A personality, these deductive team members will test your patience threshold! You will be tempted to shout, "I told you twice! Why do I have to tell you again?" But they're not doing it to upset you. They truly need to understand. Once they do understand a task, they'll know it. So, lay it out logically, walk them through until they get it.

Sensory Thinkers

A third way people learn or accept facts is through sensory experience. These are "hands-on" people. They have to see it, hear it, touch it. They have to go through the full experience. Only then will they "own" the process with you. To best mentor sensory-oriented people, give them the time they need to explore.

Deductive thinkers have to understand each step.

Sensory thinkers are "hands-on" people.

4

Encourage them to touch and feel, and they will learn faster. You can show and tell, but they must do. If you are discussing something, let them verbally process it. If you are rewriting a proposal, have them do the rewrite.

Example

Coach:

What do you think? Great report, isn't it?

Mentoree:

It sure is. And you were right about not trying to add more explanation up-front. I tried putting in the financial reasons and that only confused the situation.

Coach:

You did? Well, don't try spreading them throughout the report because it will really distract the reader.

Mentoree :

It might not cause that every time.

Coach:

You tried that too?

Mentoree :

Yes.

Coach:

Well, I'm glad I didn't tell you not to try anything else! Let's review what you have done. It sounds like a better piece of work.

Emotional Thinkers

Some minds let in information primarily through emotions. These people need to "feel good" about the work experience ... about the job process ... about their skills ... about the task outcome. If they don't, their performance will soon show it. You can often motivate emotionally responsive team members by understanding that each human being responds to one of four basic emotional needs.

> *Emotional thinkers need to feel good about the job.*

137

4

1. The need for control

Some team members respond poorly to assignments unless they feel in control of their environment. If they aren't in control, they grow uncomfortable. The way to assure someone that she is in control is to point out her "win" record. Show these team members how they are doing ... how they contribute productively. Those things all verify "control."

Example

Diane:

I've just got writer's block, I guess. I can't seem to come up with any sell lines I like.

Coach:

Well, let's brainstorm some solutions together. Point-of-purchase signage for stuffed farm animals shouldn't be too tough to have some fun with.

Diane:

It's not that. It's just that by the time the designers get finished with it, who knows if anyone will read it.

Coach:

What makes you say that? The last series you did pulled in great sales. The artists designed directly to your words.

Diane:

That time, maybe. But you never know.

Coach:

What I do know is that your words start the whole process. Without words those signs are just so much wallpaper. And I know something else.

Diane:

What?

Coach:

You and I can't draw a straight line — so we better get busy and do what we can do. Write! Your words really push the right buttons.

4

2. The need for attention

Some people won't respond very long to anything if they don't get positive attention from it. Not that they must constantly be "in the spotlight" — they simply need to know that their contributions are consistently appreciated. They need a clear cause-and-effect relationship between good performance and favorable reviews.

3. The need for love

Many people must know that the leader cares about them personally as well as professionally. These people are motivated by knowing that the coach sees "special" attributes in their characters or abilities. They need to feel that the leader is grateful for them and for the type of employee they are. Most people demonstrate this need to some degree. The downside of this need? Delivering criticism is a sensitive challenge to people who need to feel cared for. Use tact, time and tenderness when correcting these team members.

4. The need for justice or "rightness"

You will occasionally manage people who won't do anything unless it's "correct" — organizationally or culturally. These folks are much like the "deductive thinkers" discussed earlier. "Why aren't you doing the job?" you might ask one of these people. "I didn't know if I should, I didn't know if it was right," is the response. These people are not going to budge until they feel the task lines up with written and even unwritten policy. Once you assure them that the procedure is organizationally correct (and, if necessary, ethically correct), they will respond eagerly and well.

When you deal with someone who is primarily motivated by emotion, find a way to tap into her basic needs. You'll likely find the results you want. Use charged words when communicating with her.

It is more important to be human than to be important.

4

Intuitive thinkers experience "eureka" moments.

Intuitive Thinkers

The fifth way people assimilate data is by intuition. Intuition is an unconscious process that is neither rational nor emotional. Have you ever worked on something all day that didn't "click" somehow? You didn't quite get it. Then you went to bed that evening, ill at ease about the day's unsettling activity. But the next morning you woke up and ... eureka! ... you had the answer.

That's an aspect of intuition. While you sleep, your unconscious mind still processes information. Sometimes it wakes you in the middle of the night with the right answer. When you mentor people who operate by intuition, you have to give them time to grasp things. Tell them, "Hey, sleep on it. We'll look at it tomorrow. No problem." You may be surprised at the number of "eureka" moments experienced by these people.

Scientific Thinkers

Scientific thinkers must test their own theories.

The last way people process information is scientifically. To mentor these people means to let them test it, try it, experiment with it. They have to explore the information scientifically. Until they do that, your counsel is often just so much theory to them. For example, let's say you're teaching them a new computer program. If you say, "Whatever you do, don't do that because if you do, it will erase everything," their response is, "How do you know?" You might say, "Well, it happened to me. I did that and everything was gone." Don't be surprised if they come back with, "Maybe it's changed." Maybe something is different now and it doesn't work that way. Let these people experiment and try out their own theories. Set up safe situations for them to satisfy their curiosity.

Knowing that people think and process information differently, cautions you that you cannot talk to each associate the same way. How will you determine the ways your people respond to information? Observe and ask questions. The following questions can generate responses to help you evaluate which category each team member might fall into. While almost all of us are combinations of the six types, usually one approach dominates our thought patterns.

Style Analysis Questions

- Does this part of the job make sense to you?

- Does any part of the task seem unnecessary?

- Would you call this task hard? Easy? Why?

- What might you do differently to streamline the task?

- Is there anything that might better equip you to do the task?

- What part of the task appeals most to you? Least? Why?

The answers allow you to interpret how your associates think and how best to respond to them. Many times, your advice and explanations, stories and examples will do the teaching. Match their thinking styles with the way you provide information to ensure the best results.

Neurolinguistic programming is another tool to supplement your ability to understand thinking style. We are discussing how people process information and how people take in information for processing through their senses. Some are more visual. They rely on seeing it to understand what you are saying. When you use visual words — "see", "look", "picture" — they will get the message. Others rely on their auditory senses and listen for meaning. They require slower speech and words like "hear", "listen", and "sounds like" to trigger their understanding. The kinesthetic learner grasps meaning by movement. She feels, senses, gets it, in an active sense. Each of us has preferences for how we take in information. If one parallels how people talk with how they think, a mentor immediately realizes a sense of comfort and understanding with her associate.

4

The "10-60-90" Principle

The Three Key Phases of Successful Mentoring

Do you remember classes in school where you sat for what seemed like hours and repeated facts over and over? How many of those facts do you remember today? For that matter, how many of those facts did you remember two weeks after you were tested on them? Not many? Join the crowd!

You don't remember them because you were told only facts. You weren't shown how those truths could be applied in your daily life. And you weren't asked to apply that information yourself. An example of the best kind of learning we experienced as children is the art of tying a shoelace. We were first told that tied shoes made our feet feel better and lessened the chance of tripping over loose laces … then we were carefully shown how to tie those laces … and finally we were supervised as we tied our own shoelaces. Result? Information we have "owned" since preschool — and will always own.

True learning works the same way with adults. When you tell an adult how to do something, she will remember 10 percent of what you say. If you show an adult how to do something, she will remember 60 percent. But if you do something with that same adult, she will remember 90 percent or more. Mentoring is about doing and about understanding. It doesn't matter how much you can do something. Nor is it important that you demonstrate perfectly. You help the associate understand the why so that she can do it and repeat it at will — her will.

Based on those facts, the best way to teach adults is by discussing, explaining and involving. Certainly, have them do tasks. Make sure, though, through storying, that they see, feel and hear the big picture. An example is how math is often taught. People pass tests, get 100 percent and A's by multiplying, dividing, adding and subtracting. Teachers do great jobs teaching the processes of math. But the students who excel, who can transfer knowledge into real-life situations, are the ones who learned the philosophy of math, who had teachers who explained to them the fundamental principles. As a mentor, you aren't as concerned with the doing today as you are with building the foundation of their future.

The three phases of the mentoring process use the "10-60-90" principle to instruct people so they will learn and grow to their greatest potential in the least amount of time. As a StaffCoach™ in the mentoring role, there are three steps to add to the underlying understanding. First, make your associates successful; second, show them their success; and finally, make sure they understand why they are successful.

The three phrases of mentoring follow:

1. PHASE 1 — Observe
2. PHASE 2 — Participate
3. PHASE 3 — Conduct

Phase 1 — Observe

In the first phase, the person you teach observes you or someone else doing the job. As she watches, you should be answering questions. You need to answer these questions, even if they aren't asked outright.

- Why is this job important?
- What are the key components of this job?
- What are the cautions?
- What timing issues are important?
- What's in this for me?

Example

Coach:

Well, what did you think of that sales meeting, Phyllis? Pretty wild, huh?

Phyllis:

Yes, but you handled it well. I just hope I can do it half as well when the time comes.

Coach:

What part of it seemed the most difficult to you?

> *"That is happiness: to be dissolved into something complete and great."*
>
> — Willa Cather

Phyllis:

Just hearing so many problems or objections that you have to have answers for. I could never plan for all of those.

Coach:

Sure you could. All of the problems expressed today by the sales team dealt with two basic areas: existing product pricing and dealer service issues. The key to solving those problems is knowing why prices are the way they are and what programs are in place, or coming, to maintain quality service — and how we compare with the competition.

Phyllis:

Oh, is that all!

Coach:

It may sound like a lot, but you'll have all the research you need to know those things very well, and well in advance. Plus, I'm confident that you can do it at least as well ... maybe better.

Phyllis:

I don't know. Some of those guys were pretty irritated — and they've been around a long time.

Coach:

True. I've just learned not to take personally anything said in those meetings, and not to feel as if I have to leave with everyone liking me.

Phyllis:

They seemed to respect you.

Coach:

If they do, it's because I know they need to hear the truth — even when it's not what they want to hear. I just stick to the truth. Sometimes it's good news, sometimes it's not. But my mother always told me, "Never alter the truth to make short-term friends, and you'll never have long-term enemies." It's a good thing to remember in sales meetings.

4

Phyllis:

I'll remember.

Earlier you read about the importance of communicating with your people. As you show them how to do the job, you add significance to the task … you communicate your own mastery of and respect for the task. You make the associate feel that she is doing a job considered meaningful by you and the organization.

A common mistake mentors make in this phase is going through the job too quickly. If you rush your demonstration of the job, the learner doesn't have a chance to absorb what's going on — to ask the questions she may need to ask. Hurrying also leaves the learner with the impression that neither the job nor the worker is really worth your time. Slow down while you demonstrate the task. Allow the learner to see every aspect of the job and ask questions. And maintain a relaxed, friendly attitude— even if you have to repeat the task two or three times.

Think for a moment about the teachers and "inspirers" you identified back in Chapter 1 (page 24). What made them so good? What made it easy, even fun, to learn from them? Chances are your answer will be something like, "I knew I could try and fail and try again without feeling foolish or worthless." No one enjoys learning with the threat of time or performance minimums hanging over her head. Give your associate time to learn and she will give you many reasons to be glad you did. Being available to talk is a key part of mentoring.

> *Don't rush your demonstration of the job.*

Phase 2 — Participate

After you've demonstrated the job, the next phase is to have the team member do the job with you. This second phase of teaching an adult to do a task involves three points.

1. **How can the task be shared?**

   First, determine how the task can be shared. You'll both be doing part of it. It's up to you to determine how the process can be shared meaningfully and memorably.

> *To teach is to learn twice.*

Generally, it's a good idea to allow the associate to assist in the task while you perform the task essentials — not vice versa. This allows a beginning person more freedom to learn … less pressure to "get it right" the first time. For instance, if you were helping your associate learn how to paint a wall, her part of the task might be holding the ladder, keeping the brushes clean, etc.

Occasionally, a task is so tied to single-operator functions that the associate can only look on while the mentor performs it, but those situations are rare. Likewise, you don't have to be there to watch what your associate does. In the mentoring session, you can discuss what happened according to her, probe for meaning, and determine what she feels are excellent happenings and where there are opportunities for improvement.

4

Exercise

List below the tasks that someone you might mentor could participate in while learning from your performance.

Protégées Name	Task to Share	Mentoree's Assistant Job	Coach's Role as Teacher

4

As discussed earlier in this chapter (page 134), people will begin to demonstrate what category of thinking they fall into in these learning situations. If you sense the associate's need for a more "deductive" or "scientific" (or whatever) teaching style, you can tailor your instructions to that style and thereby facilitate the learning experience.

2. Does the associate understand?

Next, make sure your associate demonstrates understanding. How do you know when a person has adequately learned the task? One obvious way is to ask! Determine how much the person understands about the task by asking her to explain it to you … or even better, to someone else.

3. Is there time to learn?

Allow plenty of time for discussion and instruction. As in the first phase, don't rush the process … don't make the learner feel under time pressure to complete the task. Allow time for the training to be done well.

Phase 3 — Conduct

Once you've done the task with your person, it's time for her to fly solo. There are four questions that you, as a mentor/instructor, must resolve before you begin the conducting stage.

1. How can the associate demonstrate competency?
2. What level of competency will be adequate?
3. How much inaccuracy will be allowed?
4. When will unsupervised work be allowed?

How Can the Associate Demonstrate Competency?

In most job environments, the answer to this question will probably be something fairly subjective like, "When the manager is convinced." Much of the time that response is probably fine. Being "convinced" usually means the associate appears comfortable with the task activities and the skill level required, and grasps the logic behind the order of activities, etc.

Additionally, she has no major questions unanswered … no fears or confusion are evident.

But, for other environments, where safety or secrecy issues are of special concern, written tests may be necessary to answer this question to the satisfaction of all. Your role as a mentor is to mentally and physically ready her for greater performance.

What Level of Competency Will Be Adequate?

What specific things must occur for you to feel satisfied that the associate has truly mastered the job? Are these specific things time related? Quality related? Quantity related? If answers to these questions are critical to proper job performance, they should be formalized and made known to your associate in advance. Making sure questions like these are answered positively will affect the amount of time you spend modeling a task for her, as well as the sense of urgency associated with the mentoring process.

How Much Inaccuracy Will Be Allowed?

People make mistakes when first learning a job. How many mistakes are acceptable? What kind? No person or book (outside your own organization) can answer these questions for you — but they must be resolved. Otherwise, the teaching process is an independent, irrelevant exercise for all involved. Without some performance benchmark, however minimal, words like "quality" and "improvement" become very subjective.

When Will Unsupervised Work Be Allowed?

When will you lessen your supervision of the person and allow her to be more independent? What is the price of letting the associate work unassisted? Can you afford it? With mentoring, the associate should control the relationship.

Again, these questions demand the development of general guidelines for every organizational task attempted by your associate. The form shown here is one way to enable that process. It is an excellent job aid for you.

If at first you don't succeed, you are in the majority.

Job Phase Progress Report

Task _____ Title _____ Date Begun _____ Date Ended _____
Student _____ Coach _____ Dept. _____

1. Observing the Task	Comprehension and Competence			Additional Development Needs	Manager's Remarks
	SAT.	GOOD	EXCEL.		

2. Participating in the Task	Comprehension and Competence			Additional Development Needs	Manager's Remarks
	SAT.	GOOD	EXCEL.		

3. Conducting the Task	Comprehension and Competence			Additional Development Needs	Manager's Remarks
	SAT.	GOOD	EXCEL.		

4

Phase 1: The learner watches.

Phase 2: You do the job together.

Phase 3: You watch the learner do the job.

It's the "10-60-90" principle in action!

After reviewing these three phases, what do you think you need most to mentor someone? If you said "time," you're a fast learner! This point can't be emphasized too much. If you're mentoring the right way, you'll have moments when you become very frustrated. You'll think, "This is taking way too much time — how can I keep doing this and my own job, too?"

Be ready for those moments. Work through them by implementing the "15-5-10" formula discussed earlier on page 130, and by remembering that mentoring can be effective in only one way: by taking the mentor's time. It takes time to develop team members. And, after all, what other job is more important for a StaffCoach™ than developing team members?

Build on success. Do the following after every success:

- **Set aside time to reflect on the success.**

  Ask your associate what made it a success. Was it organizational skills, technical expertise, knowledge base, co-workers, communication skills? Talk about what worked so she can capitalize on it.

- **Ask if the success factor could be strengthened.**

  Are there other projects or relationships or knowledge that would benefit her for future actions?

- **Ask where else could she apply this success factor.**

  Are there other projects or situations in her life where she might experience the kinds of success she has just experienced?

- **Think about who else needs to learn this success skill.**

  Are there people she works with who could benefit from this skill so that the team could better work together?

As you move from teaching and guiding your associates to experiencing with and celebrating their successes, you move through a positive change process that is self-sustaining.

> *What do you need most to mentor someone? Time.*

4

Consider a cycle, moving clockwise:

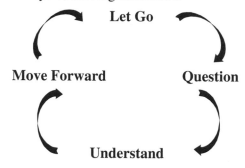

It begins as you let go; as a mentor you are giving control to your associate. It then moves to questioning. Your associate will then move on, exploring new challenges. As your associate reviews and discusses, she will be looking back to look forward.

The Outcome of Effective Mentoring

You can expect many benefits from mentoring. Your people will grow, mature, gain confidence. You will observe them gaining the following:

1. Awareness of organizational politics and culture
2. Appreciation of networking
3. Proactive approaches to their tasks
4. Eagerness to learn
5. Movement toward "expert" status
6. Attitude of "advocacy"

Awareness of Organizational Politics and Culture

In any organization, a lot goes on that isn't listed in the employee handbook. By mentoring a person whose performance is average, you can help her avoid being stymied by office politics. Through your actions, you can teach the person a consciousness of "accepted" activities that she could not learn otherwise — like who to approach with certain problems or questions and who not

to, and when and where certain activities are "the norm" or not. This doesn't mean teaching the person how to play games or how to "get around" organizational structure. On the contrary, it's like introducing a tourist to a foreign country. Nothing works better in learning an organization's culture than a guided tour by a "native."

In short, you can help your people understand what they have to know to prosper and grow in your special organizational culture and political environment.

Appreciation of Networking

Mentoring helps people see the value of "networking," not just the benefits of exchanging business cards everywhere they go or attending meetings of professional clubs to raise their industry or local-business exposure. Those things have their place in the broader context of networking, but they have little practical application in the context of day-to-day performance or productivity goals. Networking in this instance means helping your associate recognize and learn from the people in your organization most likely to help her grow professionally.

Help your people understand that interactivity and exchanging ideas with others are keys to growth ... theirs and the team's! Maybe that means scheduling time for the team member to meet with someone in the organization who once had her job. It may mean introducing your associate to the department head in charge of jobs coming to your department — or in charge of jobs coming from your area. As your associate develops an understanding of and appreciation for the "big picture," her value to the organization will increase dramatically.

Proactive Approaches to Their Tasks

Team members can't "rest on their laurels" or become content with business as usual and hope to experience significant increases in productivity. That's why you must inspire the people you mentor to become "proactive" (as opposed to reactive) about the jobs they perform. One excellent way to communicate this mindset is by practicing what Tom Peters calls the "one-idea

Teaching your mentoree about your office's politics is like introducing a tourist to a foreign country.

4

club." A one-idea club is basically the practice of two or more people meeting to analyze a competitor's approach to business. The object is to find at least one idea that the competitor is doing better than you and that you might be able to use in your own environment.

As your people complete this process, with you or others, their inclination for productivity will increase. As you go through this process, your people will become more sensitive to learning. They will look at the work environment with new insights. You'll begin to hear things like, "You know, if we did this, it might help us in this area over here." Or, "If we changed this way of working, we would probably improve that situation." That is the lifetime gift of mentoring.

Case Study

Muriel and Jeff Havens owned a small business in rural Nebraska outside Omaha called "The Berry Bucket." They and the families of their three sons tended 20 acres of blackberries, blueberries and raspberries. The business attracted a good number of seasonal, berry-picking customers, but had not grown substantially in over five years — in spite of increased advertising and new acreage (acquired by filling two of their six ponds) planted in boysenberries.

To continue to support the growing Havens clan, "The Berry Bucket" had to generate new dollars. At a monthly family meeting, it was suggested that perhaps the family business needed outside ideas. Each adult employee of the business was given the assignment of meeting with at least one person who currently operated a successful business, with the purpose of collecting advice that could translate into business growth for "The Berry Bucket."

Over the next month, six business CEOs were consulted. The businesses represented and the ideas gleaned from each are listed on the following page.

Business	Advice
Flower and garden center	Move "The Berry Bucket" into Omaha and sell berry plants as well as berries.
Savings and loan	Offer gift certificates for prepicked pints of berries, as well as for pies.
Greeting card shop	Add a gift store to the property to include local craft offerings.
Auto dealership	Offer a delivery service to the city for customers and small grocery stores.
Shopping mall	Develop year-round attractions like ice skating on frozen ponds, fairs, etc.
Marketing firm	Create a line of berry preserves with a new logo and label to test regionally.

Case Analysis

In less than three years after their decision to solicit outside ideas, the Havens' business income had increased 600 percent. A gift shop employed five additional people. Four acres of Christmas spruce and pine trees surrounded three skating ponds. And their line of Berry Bucket homemade jams was selling well in two states. Income from customers who came only to pick berries now constituted less than 50 percent of their profits.

The Havens were doing well and wanted to maximize their performance. Having no one within their own organization to mentor them, they chose outside mentors. They actively sought out people who were succeeding. They accumulated ideas, sifted through them, and identified what would work. They used trial and error, discussed what was working, and maximized successes.

Asked if she would recommend looking outside one's own work environment for new business ideas, Mrs. Havens said, "Only if you're ready to grow." The same is true for your associates — only when they are ready.

*C
A
S
E

S
T
U
D
Y*

4

Eagerness to Learn

Make sure your associates become avid and ongoing learners. Teach them to value and seek additional training — on their own or through the company. Dozens of public-seminar firms offer one-day training programs on hundreds of topics that can start your people on new roads to effective time management, problem solving, goal setting, etc. Many on-site educational firms will bring training into your organization tailored to the needs you identify. Local junior colleges, colleges and private educational institutions offer evening classes that can provide needed skills inexpensively. However you choose to support your associates' growth, nothing will assure your team's ongoing growth better than developing "professional students"!

Movement Toward "Expert" Status

Effective mentoring results in the learner moving toward expert status. As people learn, they become more than skilled professionals — they start to become specialists. By being mentored, people learn not only what they know, but also what the person mentoring them knows. It was an invaluable education process that paved the way for historical concepts like "apprenticeship." That concept transformed American business 200 years ago — and it can still do it today!

Attitude of "Advocacy"

Whenever you mentor people, you show an attitude of advocacy. It shows that you are on their side — that you want them to succeed. And the wonderful thing about this attitude is that it's contagious. People who have been mentored are more likely to mentor others. And so the circle grows.

The Treasure of Mentoring

If you've participated in the mentoring process, you know that it never really stops. The people who mentored you probably have an honored place in your memory and life — just as you will for those you mentor. Mentors are always mentors in the minds of those they help.

4

In many ways, mentoring is the fulcrum on which the roles of "coach" and "counselor" balance. Without the investment of time, sweat and commitment inherent in the role of mentor, coaching and counseling would be less credible. It is far easier to motivate or correct someone who has known you to be a sincere, caring and patient teacher.

Your mentoring style may be bizarre … your methods may not reflect the most "accepted" guidelines. But your willingness to invest yourself in the life of another person will be the key that unlocks a treasure of fulfillment and accomplishment for many people … beginning with you!

Mentors are always mentors in the minds of those they help.

Summary

At the same time that technology, performance pressures and other forces transform how organizations and their employees get things done, they also force increasing numbers of workers to reassess the role of work in their lives. The quest for a better balance between life and work, the search for more meaning in work, and increased attention to the role of relationships within the workplace are just three trends that push the role of mentor to predominance. Add to that the challenges of recruitment and retention and increased emphasis on career planning and the mentor becomes invaluable in managing the human assets.

As a mentor, you are available to your above-average performers. You teach, instruct, guide and are there for them. Many organizations have formal mentoring programs, where human resources or the department heads assign people to act as champions and advisors for the stars of the organization. Mentoring is no longer a sometimes thing for some people. It's your best bet for growing talent for your organization.

Mentoring helps people see the big picture. It is excellent for career growth.

You can help the associate understand office politics, how the organization works, what the jobs are, the mission and vision of each department and how it all fits. You can answer questions, point in different directions, and present different points of view.

4

There are elements to mentoring that are different from coaching, just as there are actions in coaching which are separate from mentoring. Respect for the individual, truth, involvement, caring and recognition are shared, though, in each approach within the StaffCoach™ Model. Mentoring is a special way the coach honors her associates. It is a total win-win situation for the organization, the coach and the associate.

Chapter Quiz

1. On what three components are good mentoring relationships built?

2. Name two of three ways to remain in control emotionally when mentoring.

3. What is the "15-5-10" formula?

4. What are the six ways people think?

5. What are four needs that drive emotionally centered team members?

6. Explain the "10-60-90" principle.

7. Name the three phases of mentoring.

8. Who is the person on your team most likely to need your mentoring?

CHAPTER 5

The Counselor Role: Confrontation and Correction

Coaching is all about you as a manager developing your people. You inspire and motivate your people who are doing their job and you mentor and guide your excellent people. The fact is, however, that those same people sometimes have problems: Performance may take a dive, they may be doing tasks in a way that is counterproductive, they may have an issue with how things are being done.

The word "counseling" in the StaffCoaching™ Model doesn't mean psychological therapy. It means confronting and correcting people whose performance is below standard. When you deal with people who are not performing at an acceptable level, you must counsel them. As with the other approaches, this does not imply a total effort; poor performance can relate to one action or one task, a part of the person's overall performance.

What constitutes "substandard performance"? The answer will vary, but substandard performance generally means:

- Ongoing attitudes or actions that willfully or ignorantly fall short of stated, written or modeled duties.

- Not meeting performance measures or goals.

- Negatively affecting others' performance goals.

> *When people are not performing at an acceptable level, you must counsel them.*

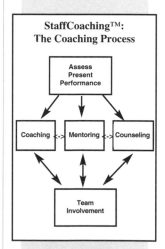

StaffCoaching™:
The Coaching Process

161

Questions to ask yourself to determine if counseling is appropriate include:

- Have the employee's duties been clearly communicated with reasonable frequency?

- Is the employee's behavior willfully or ignorantly inadequate toward these duties?

- Is the behavior ongoing?

If you answer "yes" to these questions (and assuming your criteria for "standard" performance are achievable by most people), the employee in question is probably operating at a substandard level.

Notice that "ignorance" (improper or inadequate awareness of job duties) may temporarily excuse substandard behavior … especially if the opportunity to learn has not been properly offered or presented. But lack of knowledge should only raise the training level, never lower the standard of performance.

Many managers avoid counseling for a variety of reasons. Henry Kissinger used a mandate as his means of avoidance: "There can be no crisis next week, my schedule is full." The fact is, managers dodge counseling because it does take time, and they already have full schedules. Additional reasons that you may have for not wholeheartedly jumping into this approach include the following:

- Fear of failure, not being sure what to do or say.

- Thinking that, given time, the employee will snap out of whatever is causing substandard performance.

- Rationalizing that performance isn't that bad.

- People get defensive, I get defensive, and nothing good happens.

- I didn't set the initial goals with this employee.

- I will terrorize the employee — he will think something is seriously wrong.

- Giving people time will enable them to figure it out on their own.

Add to the list "it's not my job" and that's why we have HR. You can see why so many small performance issues can explode over time into real performance problems. Discipline and confrontation are not favorites of many people. In today's more supportive and employee-centered environments, many equate counseling or correction with the old autocratic, "me boss, you do as I say" way of running a business.

Opportunities to Counsel

Knowing when to counsel is as important as knowing when to move to a coaching or mentoring approach. Many times, it is a first step in the coaching process, and will evolve to a motivating and instructing approach. When you can identify situations that require your expertise for immediate behavior change and you can act swiftly, you become more effective.

Counseling doesn't only address behavior that is beyond bad. It is not the precursor of discipline and termination. Counseling can sometimes eliminate the need for formal discipline, and certainly it is a form of disciplining or correcting performance.

Notice the variety of situations where your choice of counseling, over that of coaching or mentoring, is more advantageous.

- Reorganization, restructuring of the organization, department or work

- Layoffs, both for those who leave and those who stay

- Demotions or job reassignments

- Salary freezes, salary decreases or lowered responsibilities

- Associate unhappy with you as the boss

- Associate unhappy with a work assignment

- Associate who has a conflict with a peer

- Associate who feels stressed or burned out

- Associate who is insecure with his abilities to do the job

- Associate who has personal problems that he has shared with you

- Associate with personal problems that are affecting others' work

- Performance problems that persist
- Associate who is failing or experiencing failure

Not all associates will come to you and confide that they need help. Your ability to recognize and address competency or attitude problems before they become huge will make the situation easier to deal with. Robert Branson warns in his book, *How to Cope with Difficult People*, that any behavior not confronted will continue. Pick up on the signals, act decisively, and counseling can be swift and effective.

Anytime your people's behaviors or attitudes change, be attentive to a pattern. Consider addressing the issue with your associate if you observe:

- Decreased productivity
- Missed deadlines
- Disorganization
- Absenteeism
- Poor quality work
- Avoidance of tough assignments
- Dependence upon others to do things
- Absence from work area for long periods

Watch, also, for attitudinal changes.

- Lack of initiative
- Disinterest
- Uncooperativeness
- Defensiveness
- Little enthusiasm
- Withdrawal, quiet
- Increased complaining
- Blaming
- Not involved with team or avoiding team
- Irritability

Four Keys to Effective Counseling

Rethink the counseling part of your job as a coach. It is all about developing your people, an immediate way to honor and respect them.

Get and Give Information

In this phase, the counselor gathers relevant information from the team member and, in return, responds to the person's need to receive information.

Agree on Performance Standards

Obviously, to perform at a "standard" level for a specified task, each team member must understand and agree with the organizational definition of "standard." The counselor's job is to communicate that standard in a way that the team member can understand and explain. How can you get valid agreement? Ask questions.

- Do you fully understand the demands of this job?
- Is there any aspect of your job duties that could use some clarification?
- Do these activities seem doable to you?
- Is there anything you feel you might lack in order to do this task properly?
- How would you explain this task and the reason for it to a new employee?

Correct

The counselor implements the measures discussed, to correct the performance and raise it to an acceptable standard and above. Focus on the positive nature of counseling: to help associates become more productive ... more fulfilled.

Refer

The counselor refers the employee to the resources needed to improve his performance. Referral is crucial to performance change. Counselors don't just tell people their faults and leave it at that. They point employees to the tools (people or processes) that offer real opportunities to change and win. A positive outcome is that the associate takes responsibility for his own corrections and changes.

In some instances, effective referral may mean enrollment in a class or seminar, inside or outside the organization. It may mean asking another employee to mentor the team member in question — with special emphasis on the performance issue at hand. It does not mean disposing of the team member by pushing him off on someone else. The counselor's responsibility for the member's growth is furthered … not finished … by referral.

To better equip themselves as counselors, some leaders listen regularly to training tapes or CDs. Some read one or two books a month on subjects relevant to the managerial challenges they face. They do these things to stay ahead of the potential needs of the people on their teams — to be able to offer timely solutions to team member challenges.

Example

Bill:

I know what you're going to say: I'm doing a lousy job.

Coach:

No, I wasn't going to say that!

Bill:

You weren't?

Coach:

Of course not. I was going to ask you if there were any aspects of the job I could help you with.

Bill:

Same thing.

> *Most problems are little more than the absence of ideas.*

Coach:

It really isn't the same thing, Bill. I know you wouldn't do a "lousy job." A lousy job is when you know what to do but choose not to do it. That's not you. So what's the problem?

Bill:

I just can't seem to get my part of the assembly done on time. I don't know why. I try, but I can't.

Coach:

What part of the job do you need more time with?

Bill:

I think there's plenty of time to do the job. I see others doing it. I just get flustered or something when I see my quotas start to fall behind. I wish I were as fast as Larry.

Coach:

I'll tell you what — do you know Paul in shipping?

Bill:

Sure.

Coach:

Well, he trained Larry about a year before you came. I'm going to ask him if he'll come up here over lunch break tomorrow and tell you what he knows. Are you available over lunch tomorrow?

Bill:

Yes. That would be great.

Coach:

Paul is a great teacher. He'll know how to help. Then we'll talk afterwards. Okay?

A winning coach gets that way by investing the time necessary to find and give the information that produces winning results!

> *Why grin and bear it when you can smile and change it?*

Guidelines for Counseling

Following is a set of guides for you to use when planning an effective counseling session. Notice the many similarities with coaching and mentoring discussions.

1. Put the associate at ease through a warm approach and open body language.

2. Clearly define the reason for the discussion. If possible, have the associate state the reason.

3. Eliminate judgmental words like "should," "must," "ought."

4. Ask open-ended questions about the associate's reactions.

5. Paraphrase the content and the feelings expressed by the associate.

6. Summarize key points to clarify understanding.

7. Encourage the associate to identify alternatives to resolve the issue.

8. Be attentive to the associate's feelings and attitude.

9. Demonstrate empathy, show confidence, provide support.

10. Schedule a follow-up meeting to review and recognize progress.

Any one of these steps could encompass the entire meeting. Likewise, the meeting could fly with the associate pleased to have you acknowledge his issues. Set aside a block of private time for the session. The issues may not be able to be resolved in one setting. Judge receptiveness of your associate and the wear and tear of the meeting when allotting time. You may want to refer the person to resources or do some thinking and then come back. You may want to refer the person to your personnel or employee assistance department if the problem is beyond your ability to address.

The Philosophy of Confrontation: A Positive Approach to Negative Events

In your role as counselor, you will have to confront inappropriate behavior. Confrontation is a tough means of communication. If you aren't an assertive person, you will struggle at first. Plan, rehearse and do it. The following seven elements of confrontation will strengthen your approach.

Team Oriented

A counselor will say, "Terry, we have a problem" instead of "Terry, YOU have a problem" or "Terry, you ARE a problem" or "Terry, I have a problem." It is always "our" problem. Collaboration is your goal because you operate within a team. You're working together toward common goals … toward better results.

Positive

Confrontation is not negative but rather a positive approach to negative events. When you think of confrontation, remind yourself that the StaffCoaching™ Model is based on the concept that we are working together as a team. And as a team, we're heading toward common goals to get positive results. Performance deficiencies are normal as people learn.

Behavior Focused

Focus on the behavior, not the person. When you confront Terry, it's not like a police officer saying, "Terry, you're a bad driver. You get a ticket." It's saying, as a coach, "Terry, we have a problem. I'm going to work with you to help improve performance in this (specific) area. We're going to work it through because we want to get the best results." The idea is to help the team member perform. A counselor improves nothing by saying, "I can't believe you blew it again." As a StaffCoach™, you exist to build up, not tear down. Behavior should be your first focus … not the person!

When you think of confrontation, you shouldn't cringe.

169

Opportunity Focused

View confrontation as a tool to build the best performance possible, not as criticism. There's a difference between confrontation and criticism. Confrontation deals with issues of missed opportunity … specifically as it affects the team's ability to succeed. Criticism, on the other hand, usually deals with the individual's attitude. Criticism focuses on flaws within the person rather than on opportunities for achievement available through altered behavior.

Specific

Confrontation is very specific. Criticism tends to be more general and is frequently couched in blame or fault. When we criticize, we tend to use generalities— words and phrases like "always," "never," "everybody," "all the time."

Listed here are 10 negative (critical) remarks a manager might be tempted to make when confronting a team member about his performance. To the right are spaces for you to rewrite each phrase into a positive confrontational expression. When writing your remarks, ask yourself: Would this make me angry if someone said it to me? Does this remark close or open doors to effective communication? Does the team member have an opportunity to respond without incriminating himself?

170

5

Critical Remark	Positive Remark
Didn't you hear me tell you not to do that?	Was there something about my directions that might have been unclear?
I can't believe you actually did that!	Let's look at what happened and try to figure out what went wrong.
Why are these things always happening to you?	_____
Nobody else ever has those problems.	_____
What will it take to make you understand?	_____
If this doesn't stop, we're going to have a real problem.	_____
How can I give you a raise when these kinds of things happen?	_____
I've really had it with you.	_____
If you can't get a handle on this, we'll have to find someone who can.	_____
Why can't you do it the way Bob does?	_____

5

Cooperative

Confrontation maximizes cooperation. Confrontation says things like, "Terry, let's work together on this problem." Criticism, by contrast, says threatening, unproductive things like, "It's your problem. You better deal with it … fast!"

Encouraging

Confrontation is a specialized form of encouraging — a positive experience. Criticism is almost always viewed (especially by the person who receives it) as a negative action. Some behaviors do need to change — but change can and should be an encouraging prospect … not a discouraging one.

The Five-Step Confrontation Process

A positive attitude is especially important when you confront a problem employee. As we discussed earlier, the purpose of confrontation is to correct and help the person behave in a more acceptable manner. It is positive, not negative, and never harsh! Confrontation may never be the most pleasant thing in the world for you to do, but you can make it a lot easier — and less emotional — by applying a five-step confrontation technique to your sessions.

When the great help the small, both are just the right size.

1. Be honest.
2. Take the initiative.
3. Time the confrontation well.
4. Mean what you say.
5. Be human.

Be Honest

Don't beat around the bush. You're not doing anyone any favors if you distort the truth to save feelings. You should be conscious of feelings, but not immobilized by them. Resist the temptation to talk about anything else (the weather, the economy, "those Bears," etc.) except the uncomfortable situation in question. Don't yield to it. Hesitancy to confront the issue now may make the employee think you're not serious about the problem. Be pleasant but persistent.

Take the Initiative

Actively address the reason for meeting with the person. Work toward resolving the problem … together … in specific ways. Some counselors find it helpful to fill out the worksheet on the following page (or something like it) during the discussion. As with a job interview, however, avoid looking like you are keeping score. Give the employee a clear view of the form … even give him a copy to fill out with you, if you feel that might help keep your discussion mutually focused and controlled.

Remember, problem behavior is like a bruise. Press in the center and it's painful! Press on the outside edges and the pain is much less. But any coach will tell you that a bruise doesn't heal until its center is dispersed by heat or massage therapy. What's the moral? The problem won't go away until you deal directly with it. Don't dance around the edges.

5

Be pleasant but persistent.

5

Problem-Solving Discussion Aid

1. The problem attitude or behavior is_____
   _____

2. What makes it a problem?
   To the team _____
   To the individual _____
   To the organization _____

3. What circumstances contributed to the problem?
   _____

4. List three ways you might keep the circumstances from happening
   again.
   _____
   _____
   _____

5. Action(s) to be taken to correct the behavior
   _____
   _____

6. Consequences of unacceptable behavior
   _____
   _____

7. Consequences of correct behavior
   _____
   _____

Time the Confrontation Well

If the problem is a recurring one, try to confront the person as soon as possible after the problem behavior has occurred. However, if the behavior has made you angry or upset, delay confrontation. Initiate confrontation only when you have control of your emotions.

Mean What You Say

Don't say anything you're not prepared to back up. If you resolve to say only what you can enforce, you'll probably show little or no anger in your voice or expression. Anyone who has ever heard a parent lose control understands that anger creates unrealistic demands and makes claims it cannot stand behind.

Example

"Jimmy, I want you home faster than you can say 'jack rabbit'!"

(How realistic is that, parent?) This is the same as giving your associate an unrealistic deadline.

"John, if you don't stop talking, you'll never attend another meeting."

Is this really going to deal with John's problem — or is it your problem? Be clear in communicating the issue as well as what you want.

> *Be cool and you'll be in control.*

Be Human

Don't carry unnecessary baggage into the confrontation about how you must look or act as a counselor. Be yourself. That may mean your mouth doesn't feel like it's working right, or your left eye twitches, or your voice cracks. You're not there to look perfect but to help your team and struggling team member. And when the session is over ... even when the tone or the outcome was not especially great ... let the team member know you still value him as a person.

5

Example

"Thanks for your time, Ron. I appreciate you understanding my concerns."

"Thanks for coming, Phil. I realize how hard this is and what you must be feeling."

Remember: "Firm" is human. "Forgiving" is human. Hard and unfeeling aren't. The fact is, anytime you talk performance, even when you are focusing on behavior and not the person, it does get personal.

Learning to confront team members about performance issues as a counselor is one link in the chain of "connective interaction" between the StaffCoach™ and team member(s). Another link is working together to change the substandard behavior. One formula for that is to answer the following eight revealing questions. Your answers can clarify your approach.

Eight Ways to Eliminate Unsatisfactory Behavior

What Are the Actual Facts of the Situation?

Don't rely on your emotional recollection of the effects of the behavior — what exactly has been or is being done improperly? List the offense(s) objectively. If you're in doubt about what happened, investigate with firsthand observers. Never list what you think. List what you know.

For instance, don't settle for being told something like, "James was late twice last week in the middle of our busiest selling season." Dig a little deeper. You might discover that James arrived four minutes late on Thursday and eight minutes late on Friday, but he worked through his lunch hour both days.

> *"My players need me more when they lose than when they win."*
>
> —Jim Valvano

What Is the Specific Behavior You Want Changed?

Remember that we aren't discussing attitude. That's not behavior. If it is an attitude problem, talking about the specific behavior could reveal it and address it. For instance, addressing poor performance (behavior) by Frank could reveal his resentment (attitude) over what he considers unfair work assignments. Explaining assignment rationale and sharing its long-term benefits for the whole team could help restore acceptable performance levels.

Here again, be specific about the behavior you want changed. Is changing the behavior a one-step process, or might it require many steps over a period of time? Will Frank need short-term productivity goals that you both review weekly? Will he need outside training on the processes or equipment critical to his job? Think it through!

What Open-ended Question(s) Could Create Dialogue?

"Terry, we have a problem with your decision to delegate the initial proofs. How do you see us resolving it together?" Or, "What steps might we take to make it easier to ensure there will be no errors in the future?" These are open-ended questions. As you'll learn in the next example, open-ended questions don't put people on the defensive. They help put both parties on a healing offensive by encouraging dialogue — because they don't demand only a "yes" or "no" response.

Attitude is not behavior.

Examples

Closed-Ended (Challenging) Questions	Open-Ended (Inviting) Questions
Are you responsible for this error?	What can you tell me about this problem?
Will this step solve the problem?	What can we do to make sure this will solve the problem?
Do you understand what you're supposed to do?	Is there anything about the job that might still be a little unclear?
Are you going to meet the deadline?	What steps would help you meet the deadline?
Have you finished the Acme job?	Where are you on the Acme project?

How Can You Establish the Need for Change?

To establish a need for change, you can show how the specific behavior affects three areas.

1. The individual

2. The group

3. The organization

Consequences stated in this way etch the full impact of the behavior in the team member's mind — and put the focus on the problem instead of the individual.

> *Put the focus on the problem instead of the individual.*

Example

Mike:

I should have finished this manuscript a long time ago, Ellen. You've been more than patient. I'm sure I can finish it soon now.

Ellen:

Give me an idea how soon that might be?

5

5

Mike:

Well … I have to fit in some other client demands, unfortunately, so … I'd say three weeks. Maybe four.

Ellen:

If I give you five weeks, would you feel comfortable about committing to a final deadline?

Mike:

I can't imagine why not.

Ellen:

Good. Because after that date, the department release schedule would be badly affected — which means the entire organizational publication projection would be thrown off.

Mike:

Makes the script sound pretty crucial.

Ellen:

Right. Missing this deadline would do more than affect your chances for future scripts. It can hurt the company's bottom line.

Mike:

Then I'd better get busy. Thanks for giving me the whole picture, Ellen.

> *The smallest accomplishment is better than the grandest intention.*

Who Has Been Assigned Responsibility for the Problem?

Who is responsible directly? Indirectly? Include yourself in the latter category, because it's not just the team member's problem. It's your problem, too, not just because of organizational policy, but because you have team standards that won't be compromised.

Many managers tend to place the real concern about the employee's problems or substandard behavior "up the ladder." They make it seem as if company standards are strictly top-down. That tendency shows itself in remarks like, "They will come down hard on me if this continues … " or "The company expects you to change because ... ." Such an approach may seem to free you from being the "bad guy" in a confrontation — but it creates three deadly long-term problems.

1. The associate receives the implied message that you wouldn't object to the behavior if you were in a position to set a more reasonable policy.

2. The behavior will only become less obvious ... hidden from the unreasonable policymakers above ... but not gone altogether.

3. You'll find it almost impossible to expect compliance from that associate when it comes to future direction. Make sure he understands that.

Change happens over time.

How Will You Help to Achieve Change?

Answering this one always means a time commitment. Change happens over time. Will change mean returning to mentoring in some areas? Will it mean involving "referral" agents to more thoroughly equip the team member? Prepare your commitment alternatives in advance, and remember: No change is possible without a time investment.

What Are the Minimum Standards You Will Accept?

Decide in advance what standards are non-negotiable and define them during the counseling session. Such non-negotiables (attendance, procedures, work output, relational activities, etc.) should be in writing ... specific and measurable. If you don't have those formalized guidelines, you'll find yourself in "agreement" trouble. Know what your minimums are and why — and at least three ways your team member can accomplish those minimums.

Examples

Standard: 40 hours per workweek

Compliance options/opportunities:

a. 9 a.m. to 5 p.m., Monday through Friday

b. 8 a.m. to 2:45 p.m., Monday through Saturday

c. 8 a.m. to 6 p.m., Monday through Thursday

Standard: Meet weekly production schedules.

Compliance options/opportunities:

    a.   Set daily goals.

    b.   Review progress and problems with group leader every evening.

    c.   Hire temporary help, when needed, using money from year-end bonus fund.

Standard: Be at work on time.

Compliance options/opportunities:

    a.   Buy new alarm clock or ask co-worker for wake-up call.

    b.   Go to bed earlier and/or leave for work earlier.

    c.   Join a department car pool.

What Rewards Can and Will You Give?

Rewards aren't bribes. They are not carrots you dangle in front of team members so you can expect decent performance. Rewards are important aspects of performance management, however. We all expect positive consequences for positive effort — and it doesn't necessarily have to involve money.

Here are a few examples of the little "extras" that will communicate 1) your appreciation for positive change in employee performance and 2) your intention to respond positively to such accomplishment in the future.

Rewards

- Use of the company tickets to a sporting event
- Gift certificate to dinner and/or a movie
- Written or verbal acknowledgment in the presence of peers and/or superiors
- Personal time off
- Extended lunch or break time(s)
- Work-related gift (pen, pocket calendar, desk plant, etc.)
- Special outside training events
- Promotion
- Bonus or salary increase

Rewards aren't bribes.

181

5

Counseling Evaluation Exercise

Think of a team member who consistently delivers unsatisfactory behavior. That may mean coming to work late, goofing off or failing to complete work properly. Now answer these eight questions about the last time you counseled him.

1. Did I take the time to know all the facts?

2. Did I explain the specific behavior I wanted him to change?

3. Were my questions closed or open-ended?

4. Did I communicate the reasons the change was required?

5. Did I include myself in the problem?

6. How did I provide opportunities for change?

7. What minimum standards did I communicate?

8. Did I offer positive consequences when change occurred?

If you have thought through these questions and listed your answers, you will have developed an abbreviated action plan for dealing with any difficult behavior. Use these to debrief your sessions with your people.

Ten Essentials for Face-to-Face Counseling

You can defuse the potential for explosive counseling sessions with basic techniques. Set the stage by understanding confrontation and having some questions to answer to improve substandard behavior. You can plan around the guidelines for the session. Now consider some pressure-reducing steps you can weave throughout to hold a positive, productive counseling session.

1. Maintain privacy.
2. Avoid referring to third parties.
3. Minimize interruptions.
4. Avoid distractions.
5. Plan ahead and finish on time.
6. Control your emotions in advance.
7. Establish the facts.
8. Assess probable impact.
9. Seek behavior-related change.
10. Determine minimum performance standards.

Maintain Privacy

This rule will guarantee confidentiality and, ultimately, trust. Make sure your meeting takes place where doors can be closed. You may want to consider a location outside the office area. Assure the team member that your discussion is between you and him. Ask for that same commitment from your employee.

Avoid Referring to Third Parties as Much as Possible

Third-party references are very risky. (Example: "You know, so and so said this, so I thought it was time we talked.") They imply that you have accepted hearsay before consulting with the team member who is the object of the information. The bottom line is that third-party references (even if valid) usually succeed only in producing defensiveness.

Maintaining privacy will guarantee confidentiality.

5

183

Make Sure No Interruptions Will Occur

Be careful that you might inadvertently signal that the employee is not important. Take care of phone and people interruptions. Here's what you can do ... When someone comes to your office, notify whoever handles visitors and incoming calls that you are unavailable until a specific time. If you think you might be interrupted by an upper-management emergency, tell the team member about that possibility — and apologize in advance. When an employee sees that these precautions have been taken, he knows you believe that he is important.

Avoid Distractions

When you conduct a face-to-face meeting, choose an environment that won't distract you. Offices with no windows are best for this — especially if the windows open onto another office environment. Focus on your associate.

Plan Ahead and Finish on Time

Have you ever been told, "I need five minutes of your time," and it cost you an hour? Frustrating, isn't it? You can avoid that by making a meeting agenda. It doesn't have to be a detailed, multi-page affair — just a short outline will do. It will keep you on time and on target, while giving your team member a sense of what you want to cover and how far you are in the meeting. Also, consider attention span and the ability to concentrate. People can stay with a concept or thought for no more than 15 to 20 minutes. Group your information into palatable time frames. The ideal is to deal with no more than three points or three subjects within each 20 minutes.

If you get your voice tone under control, your emotions invariably follow!

Gain Control of Your Emotions Before You Start

Make sure your emotions are under control in two ways:
1) Make your breathing regular and deep and 2) guard your voice tone.

One effective way to chase emotion from your voice is to talk more slowly. Concentrate on speaking each word precisely and rather softly. Amazingly, if you get your voice tone under control, your emotions invariably follow!

Establish the Facts With Specific Details

We discussed this earlier. Don't speak in generalities. Broad-brush words like "always", "never", "all the time" and "everybody" only antagonize people. Make a three-point or five-point description of the specific facts before the session — and stick to it.

Assess the Probable Impact on Your Team Member

Consider reactions you can reasonably expect during your counseling session. How has the team member reacted to these kinds of exchanges in the past? What is happening in his life that might amplify or alter a "normal" response? Anticipating the team member's reactions will be valuable preparation for your session. For instance, what if you have reason to believe that Kevin's response to your counseling session might be very emotional? He may even start crying or yelling and run from your office. How can you prepare for such a possibility?

1. Document your planned session and state your concern about Kevin's possible response to your supervisor and/or your human resources director. One or both of them might have valuable suggestions for handling the session.

2. Identify the part of the meeting that is most likely to upset Kevin and defuse it as much as possible. If Kevin's poor performance jeopardizes team productivity as well as his job, practice different ways to communicate that fact accurately but sensitively.

   Wrong

   "Kevin, we can't keep you on if things don't improve."

Broad-brush words like "always," "never," "all the time" and "everybody" antagonize people.

185

Possible

"Kevin, have you thought of anything that might be preventing your ability to improve since we talked last?"

Better

"Kevin, if you had to name two or three things that keep you from performing as well as you want to, what would they be?"

3. Don't counsel Kevin alone. He should be aware that a third person will be nearby — perhaps just outside your meeting place. Having this person in the room would jeopardize the confidential environment most counseling sessions benefit from, but his presence could provide a supportive account of any incidents you anticipate.

Make Sure the Changes Are Behavior-Related

For every counseling session, the desired changes should be aimed at behavior, not attitude. That's the only real change you can measure with someone — and the only change that ultimately alters attitude.

Determine Your Minimum Standard of Performance

You must have a measuring stick. You must know what you should reasonably want. The team member can help determine how to rise to that standard, but you alone must define the standard.

The only real change you can make in someone is in behavior, not attitude.

Case Study

Reed Thurman was shipping manager for Ramco Roofing Co. His team included an office assistant, a dispatch clerk, a dock foreman, a warehouse supervisor, three forklift drivers and eight dock hands. Reed reported to the owner of the company, Lester Sisk. Reed's dock foreman, Chester Brook, was a veteran overseer. Chester's crew was divided into two teams that he changed every two or three months. The team held monthly contests that were won or lost based on the speed, neatness and accuracy by which trucks were loaded at the dock as orders were received and filled.

Over the last few months, Reed's dispatch clerk had reported an increase in clients complaining that orders had arrived with a high percentage of improper roofing materials. The problem had finally come to Mr. Sisk's attention. He held a closed-door session with Reed and ordered him to make sure the trend stopped … or else!

Reed immediately called in Chester and angrily told him to stop the team truck-loading contests. "Your guys are getting more concerned with winning a case of beer than getting the right stuff to the customer."

Chester was stunned. "These are the best guys I've ever supervised! Even when they're moving fast, they load things neat and right and … "

" … and wrong!" Reed interrupted. "No more contests, Ches. End of discussion!"

During the next three months, client complaints all but disappeared. Mr. Sisk was pleased. But dock-crew resignations resulted in six new employees. Among those who quit was Chester Brook. One afternoon, Reed Thurman's new dock foreman asked if he could change the way shipping invoices were checked on the dock.

"Why?" Reed asked him. "It's always worked okay before."

"Well," the new foreman observed, "the current way of checking a pallet of material as it leaves the warehouse could allow a forklift driver to load it on the wrong truck — especially when we are moving fast. We really should be checking material as it enters the truck."

C
A
S
E

S
T
U
D
Y

5

Reed swallowed hard. "What made you think of that?" he asked.

"Oh, some of these young replacements we've hired were seeing who could load a truck faster, and I noticed one of their forklift drivers putting a pallet on the wrong truck," the foreman answered. "By the way," he added, "if it's okay with you, I was thinking about having regular monthly contests like that to sort of build up morale. Would you have any problem with that?"

Case Analysis

1. Which of the 10 essentials of face-to-face counseling did Reed Thurman use?

2. Which did he violate?

3. Which did not really apply?

4. Which one of the 10 essentials could have uncovered the real problem and avoided the employee turnover?

5. What part did Reed's emotions play in this unfortunate scenario?

6.   What third party influenced Reed's judgment? Why?

7.   What one lesson from this case study can help you most in future counseling sessions?

Five Steps to Modifying Behavior

"Behavior modification" was a big phrase during the '70s and '80s. It remains a valuable management tool. Modifying behavior perfectly describes what a team does in order to win. You coach a team to avoid defeat, and you modify behaviors by the way you adapt each person's behavior and that of the team's. "Behavior mod" (as it is nicknamed) techniques add to an effective counseling session.

Here are five approaches to modifying behavior … yours and your employees' … that will produce dramatic victories if practiced faithfully.

1.   Gain agreement on the problem.

2.   Agree on necessary action.

3.   Identify consequences.

4.   Tie consequences to basic needs.

5,   Reward achievement.

Gain Agreement That a Problem Exists

The very first thing that must happen in any counseling session is to sit down with the person concerned and agree that "we've" got a problem. That may not be as easy as it sounds — but without it, the rest of behavior modification doesn't mean anything. If you can't get agreement that a problem exists, a resolution is impossible. Your first goal, therefore, is to gain that agreement. You want commitment, not compliance, long term.

Mutually Agree on the Action to Be Taken

This requires employee participation in the improvement process. One way to help ensure this is to ask the employee how he thinks the problem might be solved. Chances are, at least some aspect of the team member's solution can become part of a plan that you've already thought through. Results? The team member has some ownership in the solution.

Discuss the problem as "our" problem, not just the team member's problem.

Identify the Consequences of Action and Inaction

This point is a must in any improvement process. Not only should you not sidestep it, but you should ideally formalize agreement on consequences by asking, "Do we have an agreement on expectations and consequences?"

You can document the counseling session and ask for signature affirmation from the team member concerning expectations and consequences; this is useful for serious infractions. The approach you take will vary with the organization and your own style. The important thing to remember is to end every counseling session by recapping decisions and focusing on action to be taken. Talking about substandard behavior is good, but behavior that isn't targeted for specific action will never change.

Consequences must be specific.

And, of course, consequences must be specific: "If we can't see at least a 5 percent increase by this time next month, Roy, I feel we must (consequences). Does that seem right to you?" Plan ahead to figure out what consequences are right for the needs of the employee in question. It's not something you can do on the spot. Cover positive as well as negative consequences. Point to the benefits of following through on the proper behavior you have targeted.

Make Sure the Consequences Affect Basic Needs

Tie any consequences of poor performance to basic needs. The employee will continue to perform unsatisfactorily unless there is a meaningful consequence to his actions.

Examples

Consequence (Negative)	Basic Employee Need
Closer supervision	Increasing independence
No promotion	Growth and affirmation
Reduced responsibilities	Pride in achievement
Reduced income	Consistent lifestyle

No consequences will motivate any two people exactly the same way — but motivating consequences can be found for any team member. Human beings change negative behavior only when consequences encourage … even force … positive behavior.

Reward Achievement

Changing any negative behavior for long demands external motivation. As research and job interviews increasingly point out, the best motivation isn't always money. For instance, showing that new behavior will benefit the employee's leisure time, health, safety or status (through promotion or increased autonomy, etc.) often provides the needed incentive to change behavior.

5

The best motivation isn't always money.

Behavior Modification Exercise

Now, to sharpen your confrontation skills, try writing a scenario of your own. Pick a problem team member (past, present or imaginary) and write how you think you could persuade that person to respond positively to a confrontation through your use of the five approaches just discussed.

Employee name_____

Substandard behavior _____

In counseling this person, would you …

1. Gain agreement about the problem?

2. Agree on necessary action?

3. Identify consequences?

4. Tie consequences to basic needs?

5. Reward achievement?

Ask Questions That Get the Answers You Need

Have you ever tried to communicate with someone who continually gives one-word answers ("yeah" or "nope") to your questions? It may be you, and, as mentioned earlier, the right questions can be critical to understanding what motivates, troubles, inspires, angers or impresses team members. The right questions create dialogue. How? By being open-ended. To ensure these questions work, remember to be silent after asking. With no help on your part, your associate is more compelled to fill the void.

Open-ended questions are a lost art in most work environments; pressure and time encourage brief communications. Coaches give commands, often for the sake of brevity. "Tell me." "Explain to me." By substituting commands for questions, people automatically become defensive ... and dialogue shuts down.

Open-ended questions create rapport. They signal interest and concern. They don't demand a "yes" or "no" answer. They're easy to identify because they usually start with one of these words: who, what, where, when, how or why.

Open-ended questions accomplish five key objectives.

1. Minimize defensive responses.

2. Show the speaker's interest in the hearer's ideas.

3. Communicate an openness — freedom from "right" or "wrong" answers.

4. Are 100 percent more likely to stimulate conversation.

5. Create a sense of "team" ... of pulling together toward mutual victory.

5

The right questions create dialogue.

193

5

Exercise: Creating Open-Ended Alternatives

Earlier we looked at examples of closed-ended questions and at the open-ended alternatives that would encourage things like dialogue and mutual respect. Now it's your turn to provide the alternatives. Rewrite each of the questions shown here into questions that accomplish one or more of the five objectives just discussed.

Closed-Ended Questions	Open-Ended Alternatives
How long are we going to have to put up with this kind of behavior from you?	_____ _____ _____
What in the world made you do such a dumb thing?	_____ _____
Is this the best you can do?	_____ _____ _____
Didn't I ask you not to do it that way?	_____ _____
Everyone else has to suffer because of your mistakes.	_____ _____
If you can't get this right, how can I trust you with more responsibility?	_____ _____ _____
You are becoming known as a problem.	_____ _____

The ability to ask open-ended questions is vital to your success as a counselor, a mentor or a coach. Take every opportunity to ask questions. They let you tap into the unlimited resources of the people who work for you.

The Results of Effective Counseling

If you are an effective counselor, you can expect a myriad of results. Five of the most obvious benefits include:

1. **Shared ownership of goals**

   Team members … maybe for the first time … will begin to understand how performance goals relate to them individually and how to achieve those goals.

2. **New errors don't become old errors**

   Your team members will develop an awareness of what constitutes good and bad work, and will be more inclined to: 1) want to please you, 2) increase team productivity, and 3) halt negative behavior before it becomes habitual.

3. **Employees become teammates**

   Successful counseling promotes the importance of individuals contributing to the whole. Counseling reduces the individual's sense of being a "lone ranger," whether performing poorly or well. All behavior affects the team and the team members know it.

4. **Strong goal orientation**

   Counselors who experience the greatest success have helped team members leap roadblocks by setting and achieving meaningful short- and long-term goals. They teach the power of goal setting. What's that? Perhaps this power is best illustrated by recalling the old riddle: "How do you eat an elephant?" The answer: "One bite at a time."

   Good counselors acknowledge the long-term goal (eating the elephant), but focus on the short-term measures (one bite at a time) that make the final vision achievable. Once the team experiences the power of goal setting, it becomes a familiar, trustworthy team tool.

5. **Confrontations are fewer and increasingly positive**

   The good news is that effective confrontation minimizes repeat sessions.

Always work with the construction gang and not the wrecking crew.

"Action may not always bring success, but there is no success without it."

—Benjamin Disraeli

195

5

Exercise: Does Counseling Work for Your Team?

Under each of the points listed below (and discussed on the previous page), note: 1) the positive results of counseling evident in your team environment, 2) any results your team may lack, and 3) specific steps you could take to experience improvement.

Benefits of Counseling	True/False	Explain	Action to Improve
1. Shared ownership of goals			
2. New errors don't become old errors			
3. Employees become teammates			
4. Strong goal orientation			
5. Confrontations are fewer and increasingly positive			

5

Summary

Counseling is the least favorite of the three approaches in the StaffCoach™ Model and is the one most easily identified with achieving results. Done well it is a win-win situation for you and your associates.

Your people want to win and they want to be on a winning team. When you step up to below-average or poor performance and deal with it immediately, you strengthen the team and assist the associate. There are a lot of reasons why managers avoid counseling. Having guidelines and steps to follow will minimize the frustration and fear of addressing negative behaviors.

Confrontation signals a negative approach yet differs from criticism in its emphasis. The goal of any counseling session is support and recognition. The associate is important to you, so much so that you will take the time to assist him in his ability to improve. An important aspect of counseling is that, although you are counseling to help, correct and improve, the associate owns the problem and is responsible for addressing the issues.

Counseling is more promoter than police officer, more healer than henchman, more director than dictator. You aren't trying to push everyone into the same behaviors and the same molds. You counsel to help people see where they fit and what they must do to fit. You maintain their best interests by taking care of the organization's objectives and needs. Molding and shaping are all about increasing your people's abilities to stretch. As they develop flexibility, they will better cope with the exponential changes that are bombarding them in this new workplace.

The values of the StaffCoach™ are the values of the counselor. Your emphasis is your people.

> *A counselor doesn't push "square" team members into "round" organizational holes.*

5

?

Chapter Quiz

1. What are the four keys to effective counseling?

2. Name three of the five steps to positive confrontation.

3. List eight ways to eliminate unsatisfactory behavior.

4. Name five of the 10 elements of productive counseling sessions.

5. Who is one team member you look forward to "molding" over the next few months?

C HAPTER 6

Integrating the Individual and the Team

When you are coaching individuals, it is easy enough to specify desired performance, keep a log and connect with them regularly. There is no problem determining how much more or less you should encourage, instruct and direct. Your job, though, as a manager is not to manage results but to manage the aspects of performance that cause those results. That's where your team emphasis comes in.

Integrating your associates' strengths and capabilities so that the team reaches optimum performance requires similar yet different skills on your part. Absolutely, the guidelines for coaching are applicable. Setting expectations, defining measures, supporting and praising are invaluable to the team. Broadening the team's view is effective and correcting work is necessary. Merging individuals into a collaborative team requires some real balancing.

There will be some times when what is good for the team may not be the best for an individual. You may have, for example, a very creative individual on the team who just brought you a great plan for reorganizing the data files. Her idea would win the company the "Outside the Box" award of the month for innovation. Implementing it, however, would be a depressing experience for two of your other specialists who have been researching some different approaches for the same result. Recognizing your associate for her great idea while not accepting the action requires mental agility and verbal acuity (not to mention some tap-dancing thrown in, perhaps). Balancing individual needs and team needs is as tough as looking at the short-term and long-term goals you are constantly reassessing.

A second balancing act with regard to integrating your individual and potential stars into a strong team deals with the approaches and the steps of the StaffCoaches™ themselves. What you have been doing for and with the individual team members — coaching, mentoring, counseling — also needs to be done with them as a whole. Talking to a group of people is a challenge when each listens differently, has different points of view and is emotionally charged at different levels. The tips and techniques work; the orientation and adaptation on your part cause success. StaffCoaching™ has as its focal point staff, or your team, coaching the team of individuals.

Group vs. Team

Groups have been around since the beginning of time; human nature draws people to one another. Group behavior ranges from supportive to chaotic, from disaster to success. Many managers are fine with group performance. For the StaffCoach™, though, it is increasingly evident that groups that experience the highest output are those that have bonded into a team.

A main distinguisher between a group and a team is their orientation to one another. A group is two or more people working in proximity, each doing her own thing to accomplish a goal. A team shares the same goal. Its work is dependent upon each team member for the final results. An example is the curriculum team at National Seminars. While it is a group of people with different accountabilities — one laying out materials, one proofing, another editing, another administering tasks — none is successful without the other. The final product, whether book, CD or electronic presentation, cannot be completed without the team's integration of talent.

The coach's job is all about getting results. You do that by building your team, individual talent upon individual talent. You balance the multiple needs, recognizing one and minimizing another to integrate them into a unit. Taking care of your

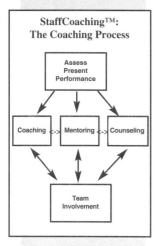

StaffCoaching™:
The Coaching Process

Assess Present Performance

Coaching Mentoring Counseling

Team Involvement

6

associates in a holistic focus is what makes the team strong. Developing individual team members so they compensate for and support one another makes them a team. As individuals improve, the team improves. The result of moving among your roles of coaching, mentoring and counseling is what your team produces — productivity and job satisfaction.

Ask employees today what motivates them to join one organization over another and a top response is to be able to work with the team. Integrating your individual associates into the team requires the same skilled approaches of the StaffCoach™. Shared values, common goals, constant rewards and satisfaction take a group and shape it into a top-performing team.

Instill Team Vision

The greatest outcome of successful StaffCoaching™ is a team that works together for inspired performance. Given the right vision and guidance, any team can achieve new levels of performance. In a visionary environment of trust and commitment, people develop strengths they never knew they had.

Every truly great coach in history had a vision … a dream of what a team could achieve … whether that coach was Roy Williams, Martin Luther King, Martha Graham or Walt Disney. The coach who integrates individual performers into one cohesive team with a common view is the coach who gets results. Great coaches communicate that vision to their teams in a way that inspires.

Only with vision can you have a winning team.

For you to be an outstanding StaffCoach™ and build a team that achieves inspired performance, you need to have a vision, and then you need to share it. Every person on your team must feel that she has a personal stake in the vision. Your role as coach gives your people a vision that meets their needs and motivates them to be the best they can be. Having an inspiring goal keeps the team on target, but the excitement and energizing addition of vision draw people in.

Without a vision, the team is just a work group, a "unit," with each person doing her job ... getting through the day. Simultaneously, as you develop your people's potential individually, integrate them into a team. Do that by giving them a common vision. You can take four actions to shape that vision.

1. Write out your highest hopes.

Don't limit yourself at this stage. Involve the whole team. Set your sights high ... your most ambitious expectations ... your most cherished dreams for your team. Make your vision one that will inspire people and assure them they are working for something great!

Examples

- To be the best team this organization has ever experienced.

- To provide the greatest opportunities for advancement.

- To provide superior customer service by a balanced approach to work and life.

2. Link your vision to organizational goals.

How does your vision line up with the corporate direction ... with your market ... with your budget? If you create a vision that's out of sync with these key business elements, you and your team are setting yourselves up for frustration.

Let's say one of your department goals is to increase product quantity, but the driving division goal is to increase quality. You could be in the unenviable position of receiving team reprimands even when your team members exceed your goals! Always make sure your "mission" or "vision" is based on and complements the larger corporate objective:

- To operate as a totally self-directed team within the next 18 months.

- To enroll every member of the team in at least two job-related educational experiences every year.

- To achieve and sustain the highest level of productivity in company history.

"Vision is the art of seeing things invisible."
— Jonathan Swift

202

- To have a 100 percent accident-free work record for one full year.

- To operate for 90 days without receiving one customer complaint about department service.

3. **Develop a strategic path for reaching your vision.**

   Identify the necessary steps and resources you need. Identify the tools your team will need to work effectively toward achieving your vision. For instance, if your goal is to increase sales by 20 percent during the third quarter, list the specific "behaviors" that will accomplish that, such as: Make 10 more calls per day ... Attend "How to Sell Effectively" seminar ... Develop new leads from old customer referrals. Where do these "behaviors" come from? They come from your team. Brainstorming sessions with your team to develop action steps not only create a stronger sense of unified purpose, but also give each member ownership in the resulting plan.

   Once you've listed the steps to your goals, ask your boss to review your written recommendations. Get her ideas ... and approval.

4. **Implement your vision.**

   Once you have input from team members and approval from your leadership, transfer the "ownership" of the strategic plan to your people. Then get out of their way! You show your willingness to provide ongoing, positive and constructive feedback — and, when it's time, to provide direction and support. Your team knows that you endorse reasonable risk taking and that failure isn't terminal as long as productive learning results. They learn this constantly through your StaffCoaching™.

Brainstorming sessions create a stronger sense of unified purpose.

6

Recognize the Potential for Team Trouble

To keep your team running smoothly, stay alert to signs of trouble. These are similar to the signals to watch for with individuals who may need counseling. If you notice them in your team, they could be even more dangerous since they potentially affect everyone's performance.

Here are six common signals employees may send indicating they are losing momentum on the job.

1. **They are falling behind.**

   When job progress slows down because team members can't seem to get their work done on time, check your lines of communication! Either a) you aren't inspiring and motivating through regular team meetings, b) your associates aren't telling you about specific productivity or workflow stumbling blocks, or c) general unspoken resentment exists among team members. Immediately start a dialogue to discover what is happening.

2. **Team member actions or plans are vague.**

   Employees have difficulty explaining how specific jobs will be accomplished. If you aren't getting clear explanations, immediately probe. Initiate a meeting to clarify actions through team brainstorming sessions, new job or project descriptions, or clarified expectations for procedures and deadlines.

   Coach:

   Well, this looks good, Barb. I think you should probably go with it. But how will you hand off to shipping when Donna has her job finished? That looks kind of critical.

   Barb:

   It really shouldn't be any problem. Donna has had that part of the project under control for a long time.

   Coach:

   You're probably right. But you've got a couple of new wrinkles that might confuse her. It sure would me. Does she know about them?

When job progress slows down, check your lines of communication.

6

Barb:

Well, generally.

Coach:

How can you get specific with her? I wouldn't want you to get all the way to Donna's department before discovering a glitch. Other than that, let's do it. Great job!

3. **Employees become overly optimistic about projects.**

   This is difficult to detect, especially because optimistic enthusiasm is exactly what coaches like to hear! But watch out. Team members may bite off more than they can chew in the interest of pleasing you or making the team look good. The danger is that unrealistic optimism sets up your team for failure — maybe even repeated failure. Make sure someone who is objective monitors project goals, and make sure your people know they don't have to be super-humans to be superstars on your team!

4. **Employee anger or stress increases.**

   Reasons for irritated team members can be many and varied, but you can usually identify them through counseling. You may discover a well-concealed dispute between two or more members that has team-crippling side effects.

   Maybe general dissent exists over a new policy or procedure. Ask questions — and ask as many team members as it takes until a consensus begins to surface. Is there a grievance, condition, event or personality that runs like a thread through each counseling interview? Does the name "Joanne" surface repeatedly in a negative way? Does the plan to relocate the department to another floor keep coming up? Or the companywide salary cut? The starting point for uncovering widespread dissension is talking to your team.

5. **Absenteeism**

   Absenteeism is also a strong signal that something is wrong. As in No. 4 above, getting involved with your people and pinpointing likely causes of the problem are critical to finding solutions. In the meantime,

6

> *Team members may bite off more than they can chew to please you or to make the team look good.*

> *Absenteeism is a strong signal that something is wrong.*

205

consequences for absenteeism should be reviewed. If absenteeism is widespread, consequences apparently aren't strong enough.

6. Avoiding contact and/or conversation

When one of your team members starts avoiding you, the reasons can be many. Among them might be the following:

- General unease in the presence of authority.

- Performance anxiety — fear of communicating in a way that isn't "good" or adequate.

- Fear of being asked to do something.

- Dread of being asked what she has done about a specific task.

- Guilt over real or imagined poor performance.

The remedy for all these has its roots in coach "contact" — constant, consistent contact. The more time you spend with team members, the more you're viewed as being genuinely interested in promoting individual success — and the fewer the negative incidents will be. As you become human and accessible, your team will become open and free of distrust.

When the entire team seems to avoid you, however, the probable causes can be quite different.

- A problem exists and your anticipated solution is not what they want to hear.

- A decision, assignment, attitude or action of yours (real or rumored) has communicated an anti-team message.

- An unpopular procedure or policy "from the top" has made you guilty by association.

You can respond to these situations in one of three basic ways including:

1. Do nothing — wait until someone shares the problem, then address it. This approach works best when you are virtually positive the problem involves something you can't change, such as a companywide policy

about shorter lunch hours. In time, such unrest almost always diminishes and even disappears. Confronting the unrest before it runs its course can fuel fires that would have otherwise extinguished themselves.

2. Meet with key team members, individually or together. Ask what's going on and why. List the facts and (now or later) deal with each fact one at a time, asking for input and ideas. When these key members are satisfied that either a) you are aware of the problem and are taking steps to work with them to resolve it or b) your joint solution is acceptable, they can give the results of your meeting to the other team members.

3. Call a team meeting. Clear the air. Invite honest, open discussion about any problems that team members may see as unresolved. Your willingness to meet issues head-on will be more important than your ability to "fix" things on the spot. Just listen. Take notes. Let people talk. Discuss solution options … even assign "solution teams" if possible.

In every instance, with an individual or a group, the key to dealing positively with defensiveness or aloofness is the same: Face the problem at the first opportunity. When your team sees that you want positive, constructive confrontation, they will increasingly tend to speak their concerns … and be less and less likely to hide them.

6

Face the problem at the first opportunity.

Case Study

Linda Benchley's team of computer technicians worked with some of the most expensive inventory at MacMasters Inc. Eighteen full-time technicians formed the nucleus of the MacMasters IS department. They were divided into three teams of six members each, with each member specializing in different PC configurations and networks.

When one of the teams began missing expensive parts, Linda and the team leader met to discuss the problem. The team leader, Rob, reluctantly admitted that he suspected one of his people of theft. Linda and Rob carefully documented their meeting and met

C
A
S
E

S
T
U
D
Y

with the company's owner before meeting with Becky, the team member Rob suspected.

Becky was well-liked by every employee and was a favorite with regular MacMasters customers. Her special talents with system repairs as well as her quick sense of humor made everyone appreciate her. Becky's brother, Mark, was also a technician in the service department. When Linda and Rob told Becky about the disappearance of parts from her area, she hotly denied any wrongdoing. Linda carefully explained that no one was being accused — only questioned for any information they might have.

Over the next six months, more parts disappeared. When questioned again, Becky claimed to know nothing about the disappearance. Then Rob saw her slip a new memory board into her briefcase before leaving work one day. When Becky was dismissed three days later, she returned the parts or the dollar equivalent of everything she had taken in order to avoid prosecution. Out of deference to Becky's brother, Mark, and out of concern that customers might hesitate to trust their hardware to MacMasters technicians, as well as possible legal ramifications, the company did not tell service department personnel why Becky was dismissed.

As a result, Linda and Rob became the target of much gossip and ill will. Morale and productivity in Rob's group plummeted, and absenteeism rose dramatically. The person Rob hired to replace Becky met with such a cool reception from the other team members that she resigned after only three weeks. Finally Linda decided something must be done. After discussing it with Rob, Linda met with Mark to tell him why his sister was dismissed and to ask his permission to note only the specific, documented reason for the termination. Having suspected the reason for Becky's departure, Mark quickly consented.

In a group meeting, Linda led a three-part discussion to:

1. Announce the reason for Becky's dismissal.

2. Assign a committee to develop a plan to prevent similar problems in the future.

3. Announce a "MacMasters Night" at the ballpark, complete with tailgate party.

6

Within three weeks, the service department was back up to speed. The "Houdini Team" (as their peers affectionately named them) devised a logical, nonthreatening theft-prevention procedure … Becky's first replacement was recontacted and rehired (with explanations and apologies) … Mark dealt personally with Becky's past customers to assure them that the level of expertise they had come to expect had not dropped.

MacMasters Inc. returned to normal.

Case Analysis

1. Based on what you have learned so far in this chapter, was Linda right to withhold the facts about Becky's dismissal? Why? Why not?

2. What could she have done differently?

3. How could she have avoided the morale problems you read about?

4. Which of the six signals of lost momentum were communicated by service department members?

5. How did Linda respond?

Chances are that Linda left this unfortunate encounter a much wiser leader. It's never a good idea to withhold information critical to team action and interaction. In this case, everything worked out all right. But only a successful meeting and a great plan going into it saved the service department. Other areas that were impacted included confidentiality, privacy, legal and company policy. What could have been easy to handle with one individual was much more challenging when dealing with a team of individuals. There is no such thing as secrets with a team. Respect, consistency and clarity are what works.

Commitment and Mutual Support

You make commitment possible for the team when you take individual goal setting to the team level. Commitment cannot be forced. It is self-generating and develops through involvement. What you do with each associate can be paralleled with the team. Rather than you having a meeting, stating each person's goals and showing how you pulled them all together, employ the same strategy with the team.

Let your team contribute to its success. Actively involve team members in the goal setting and the problem solving, as a team. Developing a sense of ownership together will expand their potential. One important action team members can take is shaping their own systems and methods. Depending upon their skill and experience, you can facilitate, guide or correct these decisions. The point is to allow team members to shape the direction together.

There are several actions you can take as the team develops its methods of integrating talents. You can:

- Ensure team goals are achievable and challenging so that results are appropriate for the organization while satisfying the individuals.

- Assist in balancing the complexity of measures and controls with workable checkpoints so that there is accountability.

- Participate in discussions so that pros and cons are weighed.

- Assess what cooperation and support the team will need.

- Follow the progress of the work to reward and reinforce results.

When problems occur or personalities clash, you can revert to your mentoring or counseling role. The steps in working with your team parallel problem solving with an individual.

1. **Communicate what appears to be the problem.** This may not be the actual problem, but by bringing the issue into the open you can start the process of dealing with it. The number one reason problems aren't always solved is that people are dealing with the wrong problem. An example: There is a negative attitude that makes coming into the office unpleasant. There is a lot of frowning and mumbling; no one seems to be looking at each other.

2. **Discuss what is happening.** Gather facts, ask people's opinions. This lets you and the team identify what is the real problem. The team may respond: "It isn't any fun around here. Everybody is stressed. The deadlines for three projects are hitting the fan, and now there is more being dumped on us."

3. **Redefine the problem.** Take the facts and input of the team and restate what really is the problem. The earlier this is done, the easier it is to deal with the real issues. You might respond to the above example with: "So deadlines are clashing and we didn't anticipate the additional projects coming at us? This is adding to stress and frustrating everybody."

4. **Discuss alternatives for dealing with the problem.** Ask the team their ideas for handling this. This step underscores the necessity to plan your meeting. Consider having separate meetings so that people have time to think. A caution: A brainstorm session becomes ineffective after about five minutes of spilling out ideas. Likewise, negating any idea during the brainstorm tends to stifle the flow of ideas.

5. **Decide how to address the problem.** Again, this might be accomplished in one meeting, going through Steps 1

6

6

through 6, and it might take a couple of meetings, with a time interval for the team to collect their thoughts. Important in this step is not pushing the solution you know is a winner. Get a consensus. Help the team in seeing the big picture, the implications or impact of their solution on other departments or the organization. Focus them on costs. Example: If one of the alternatives for the above problem was to tell the marketing department to reduce their campaigns, that would be totally unfeasible. Their results are based on customers and customers come through campaigns. Point the team toward what they control and what they can affect.

6. **Commit to action on the solution.** When the team agrees to a solution, an action plan with detailed steps best guarantees success. An example of one solution for the above is to assign one team member the task of getting a month-by-month projection of marketing activities. Have another team member project-manage various tasks and stagger the due dates. Another solution could be to have team members monitor stress levels and to make sure they add a fun diversion into the schedule or a prize at the end of a grueling stretch.

7. **Follow up.** Check the results regularly. With the team, monitor whatever solution is chosen. Acknowledge what works and build on success.

A Checklist for Responding to Team Troubles

Before you act on any apparent problem, especially when things seem to be out of control, always outline a plan. Great coaches don't react to situations. They give themselves time to think a problem through. One of the many reasons that Shirley Tilghman, a pioneer in mapping the human genome, was chosen as Princeton University's first woman president was her strength in pulling dissenting opinions together. She acted, not reacted, after listening and studying each position. Others might respond on impulse with their first thoughts or react to a time pressure. A good coach plots exactly what course is needed to remedy the situation.

To help you keep a cool head in a crisis, answer these eight questions before you make a move.

1. **What are the facts of the problem?**

   Be thorough with this one. Do your homework. The act of listing the facts can be the shortest route to revealing an obvious problem.

   A form like the "Fact-Recap Sheet" shown here provides a simple but solid way to organize your thoughts and shape a plan of action.

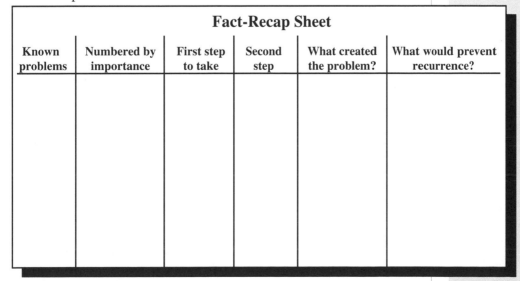

Fact-Recap Sheet					
Known problems	Numbered by importance	First step to take	Second step	What created the problem?	What would prevent recurrence?

6

2. What behaviors are at issue?

As learned in Chapter 5, always focus on behavior, not attitudes. Identify the specific action (or inaction) causing the problems. Even if Jill did the task grudgingly, she still did the task. If Jill made a mistake and accidentally didn't do the task, she didn't do the task. Certainly, the employee's attitude counts. Anyone would rather coach the team member who wants to do well but failed. But when it comes to immediate problem solving, it's the outcome, not the intent, you must focus on.

3. What are the consequences if things go unchanged?

Sometimes it's smarter to ignore a situation and see if it works itself out. You don't have to "rescue" everyone and resolve every situation. Occasionally a negative situation can be its own consequence … its own deterrent to the problem happening again. Or maybe the problem is so small that consequences could cause more problems by drawing attention to it. Great coaches keep a finger on the team pulse … without keeping the team under their thumb. An ineffective approach is to ignore an issue hoping that it will resolve itself. Act or don't act based on strong assessment of the individuals and the team. Jill's attitude, in the above example, could spill over to the team. Like the effect of negativity that Cherie Carter-Scott notes in her video, *Negaholics*, Jill's attitude could contaminate the team.

4. Does the problem affect immediate objectives?

What jobs are in progress? Could this problem hurt them? If the answer is "yes," then problem does jeopardize immediate objectives and you must mobilize all your energies to pinpoint the problem's source and a solution for it. If the problem doesn't jeopardize a project in progress, finish the tasks at hand before turning your attention to the disruption.

It's a little like firefighters putting aside 10 good hoses to fix one leaky hose while the warehouse burns down. Prioritize your response to the problem based on the threat to your most immediate goal.

5. How does the employee problem affect the long-range team goal?

Asking yourself this question will help you put in perspective the behavior in question. The answer will provide a strong rationale when confronting and correcting the offender(s). How? By helping the employee see that her behavior matters not because of how it matches your ideals as the leader but because of how it affects the organization's potential for success. That's because the organization's mission or vision results in goals. Those goals and objectives reflect principles such as teamwork, integrity, respect for people and candid communications. Achieving the goals means behaving in a way that complements the principles.

Counterproductive behavior hurts, not just the offender's organizational standing but the organization itself — you, the team, everybody. It's one thing for a team member to cost you a game — but that person must understand that her behavior can ultimately jeopardize the team's entire season! People do get fired for someone else's actions.

6. What are the benefits of changed behavior?

What are the benefits of changed behavior to the project, the policies and to the persons involved? You and your team members need to know what's in it for everyone if the problem goes away. That doesn't mean you must bribe a team member into compliance. It merely means showing the team member the logical conclusion of current vs. changed behavior. Pulling the entire team into rewarding change can have long-range, continuous benefits.

For example, failure to stay alert on the job means a faulty part gets by ... which means a product will not perform properly ... which means customers' lives are compromised or endangered ... which means the company's reputation is tainted ... which means sales plummet ... which means people get laid off.

On the other hand, when faulty parts are caught and reworked, team quality rises ... consumer loyalty and trust increase ... sales climb ... people keep their jobs and bonuses are given!

Surprisingly often, problem behavior is also ignorant behavior. When team members fully understand the ramifications of behavior, bad and good, the motivation to stick to company standards or work together is much greater.

7. Am I in control and ready to discuss this situation?

Only discuss a problem when you have control of your emotions. Too much damage can be done otherwise. If necessary, take a day or more to pull yourself together before acting on a problem. While it's important to respond quickly to improper behavior, there is no gain if you risk shattering a long-term solution by saying angry things you can't retract.

8. How can I support this employee and the team?

This is not always the first question that most coaches ask themselves when they prepare to respond to problem behavior. Answering it may not produce an immediate change, but it can promote long-term change. Tip: Start with the end in mind. Consider the optimal result you are striving for. Meaningful support is almost always long-term — such as assigning a mentor to help the employee learn or a coach to assist in improving, or giving additional training to help boost performance.

Supporting employees by helping them start positive behavior, not just stop negative activity, instills more company loyalty than any other single employee benefit — including salary!

"Look Before You Leap" Checklist

Use this checklist to answer these questions before confronting an employee's problem behavior.

Question	Answer	Likely Employee Response	Your Response
1. What are the facts of the problem?			
2. What behaviors are at issue?			
3. What are the consequences if things go unchanged?			
4. Does the problem affect immediate objectives?			
5. How does the employee problem affect the long-range team goal?			
6. What are the benefits of changed behavior?			
7. Am I in control and ready to discuss this situation?			
8. How can I support this employee and the team?			

6

Focus the Team With Shared Priorities

Great coaches guide their teams to do the right work. Things are easier when tasks are clearly prioritized. In many companies, management may feel in control but the employees don't at all. Employees aren't sure which tasks have top priority because everything is "hot," and the team thus loses its synergistic strength.

As a coach, you can create an atmosphere that lets you integrate their work in an orderly, prioritized way. It is your job to protect them from being abused by the system or assaulted by conflicting goals and too many directives.

Five essential steps for prioritizing team responsibilities include:

1. **Identify and minimize "hot" projects.**

    If you've ever had someone give you a job marked "urgent" and then another marked "urgent" and still another marked "urgent," you know what eventually happens. You ignore the word "urgent." It's like the boy who cried wolf. People must know what the real priorities are or they won't do anything. Distinguish between urgent and important. Urgent, like crisis, means do immediately. Important is that which gives value to the team output. While urgent work must get done, planning makes sure that what's important gets the team's attention.

2. **If the team deals with multiple bosses, coordinate priorities.**

    Don't force the team member to choose which boss she will please next. Come to an agreement with other managers about how priorities will be handled and then communicate this to your employee. If an urgent exception arises, don't expect your employee to handle it. Work it out with the other managers before handing the project over to the team member. Coming to such an agreement doesn't take long to do — not nearly as long as it takes to train a new employee to replace the one who quit because she couldn't take the pressure any longer. You can trust your individual associates to make their own decisions, but help the team avoid these conflicts by working with your peers.

3. **Share the reason for changes — beat the "grapevine" to the punch.**

   The funny thing about the grapevine is how unfunny it can be. It encourages unfounded speculations like, "I bet this change is so they can cut jobs." The first thing you know, the "official" word is that the company is cutting jobs. Panic erupts in your team! The moral: You control the information your people get. Be up-front and honest with them from the start. Ask whether they have any questions, and answer them. Put their minds at ease so they can focus on their work and not on the rumors.

   A word of caution: If you get involved with the grapevine, or listen to rumors, you are supporting them. No matter how helpful a little inside knowledge might appear, if you listen to gossip, then you gossip. It erodes your trust and credibility. Three ways to handle gossip follow.

   - Tell the person who brings it to you to go with you to the person involved so you can check it out.

   - If the person declines, ask if you can use her name to go to the person involved to check it out.

   - If the person declines, drop it. A sad truth: Bad news and bad situations resurface just like the postman who always rings twice.

4. **Encourage team problem solving.**

   The key to getting employees to work like a team is getting them to think like a team, with team goals … team communication … team recognition. The best way to start building this team thinking is to set goals that can be met only through teamwork. You might set goals for increasing group output or designing new procedures that will make everyone's jobs easier. As much as possible, let the team participate in the goal-setting process.

   Ask everyone to take part in a brainstorming session. As with the problem-solving steps noted earlier, ground rules should be a) everyone is encouraged to contribute and

There is no limit to how much good you can do if you don't care who gets the credit.

219

b) there's no such thing as a "bad" idea — at this phase. Later, after all ideas have been listed, the group can select the idea most likely to succeed. This approach helps team members listen for one another's good ideas and gives everyone a chance to contribute to a team solution without fear of criticism.

When it comes to facilitating the team's ability to handle its own problems, the best way is to simply do that: facilitate, don't solve. Instead of suggesting or telling a solution, revert to your StaffCoach™ questioning ability: How do you see it? What could you do? Think about what you just said. Do this enough and they get the idea: It really is their problem.

A good team always can accomplish more than any one individual. Once employees learn the benefits and ways of working together, they'll integrate their strengths and talents to accomplish results.

5. **Build in rewards for achievement.**

When your schedule is so tight you can't eat lunch without feeling guilty, the day is not only less productive — it's no fun. Team members experience the same sense of drudgery — and they are often less free to step off the treadmill (by delegating tasks, etc.) than you are. Fun is a major recruitment plus in today's marketplace where organizations are vying for the best talent. Potential team members question recruiters about the environment they will be entering: What is the team like? Who are the stars? What can I learn? How do they balance work and home? What do they do for fun?

Fun and celebration are StaffCoach™ tools. They can pull the best talent into your team, provide the light at the end of a stressful time, and bring the team together into an integrated unit. Laughing is a bonding experience. The potential for errors, low morale and employee burnout is great in today's high-pressure world. Regularly consider how you can provide team relief from a priority-intensive schedule. Here are a few suggestions.

"Common sense is very uncommon."

— Horace Greeley

6

220

- **Take a team to lunch.**

  This event could mark the end of a successful project or just a fun and unexpected surprise.

- **Give the team tickets to an event.**

  Get tickets to favorite events — the arts, sports, a circus — and offer them as ongoing awards for excellence.

- **Traveling trophy.**

  A funny poster, a small loving cup … anything can serve as a "team of the week" award. Will the current team or individual awardholder keep the trophy next week? Whose performance will win it next week? Watch your people have fun with these kinds of questions.

- **Family fun.**

  Plan a picnic, bowling party or a get-together where family and friends of team members can unwind and interact in a nonwork environment. A great reward for their growing effort and a great way to bond a team together!

- **Food day.**

  Designate a day for the team to bring fun foods to the office, and let them use shared breaks to gather round the treats and talk about work, the day, their lives or whatever.

- **You name it.**

  Be creative! What would you like to look forward to if you were a member of your team?

- **A twofer reward.**

  Recognize someone with two of something — two bags of microwave popcorn, two packs of gum — for the double effort they gave.

- **Switch shoes.**

  Do someone else's job for a day or an hour, and let her do yours.

6

- **Give a creature comfort.**

  Contribute a fan for the office, a radio to use.

- **A new mug**.

  Give a new mug with a humorous or serious recognition printed on it.

- **A bouquet of balloons.**

  Personally deliver it to the team's area.

- **"Let them eat cake."**

  Treat them with a special cake.

- **A nonbirthday party.**

  Celebrate no one's birthday.

There is a story in the book, *In Search of Excellence*, by Peters and Waterman, about a company that desperately needed a technical advance for it to survive in its early days. Late one evening, a scientist rushed into the president's office with a working prototype that was just what they needed to keep the business afloat. Dumbfounded at the elegance of the solution and wanting to reward the scientist, the president started rummaging through his desk drawers. He leaned over to the scientist and said, "Here!" giving him the only thing he had — a banana. From then on, a tradition was started, and a small "gold banana" pin has been the highest accolade for achievement at that company. The point: bananas work. What's your idea?

A corollary to that story: Tom Peters has been mentioned in this book several times. Do you recognize Robert Waterman? Or perhaps Nancy Austin, another co-author of Peters'? Why is it that Tom Peters is instantly known but not his associates? Consider that when you give out rewards. Do you want to accelerate one person's performance or career? Do you want the team to be known throughout the organization and extolled for its achievements?

Exercise

In your workplace, what's the greatest hurdle in encouraging team members to do "the right work right" and integrating their efforts? How can you use one of the techniques discussed to keep your staff focused on the job and increase their performance? Choose an area you want to improve and start planning for it today. For instance, you might want to circulate a memo whenever a change is announced, so everyone gets the information at the same time. Or you might want to develop and e-mail a daily list of priorities for each person on your staff. Maybe initiating team recognition would add to the individual activities you already offer. Whatever you decide to work on, make it specific and tangible.

Here are some simple but revealing questions to help you anticipate problems, design preventive measures and put strategies into action.

1. What areas currently fragment your team's work effort?

2. Based on the techniques you've just read, what's the most obvious way you could keep your staff focused and energized?

3. What specific steps will that take?

4. Which team members will be involved?

5. When will you start, and how will you measure your success?

6

Right Thinking About Team Purpose

In any leadership setting … in any workforce … two points of view can apply to the primary purpose of the team. One philosophy says the main goal of the team is to solve problems. The other approach says the purpose of teamwork is to improve performance. StaffCoaching™ states throughout that the one goal of the coach is results.

Which point of view lines up with the StaffCoaching™ Model and your own actions? Improving performance. As a coach, you encourage, energize, motivate, guide, and solve problems. You take actions and plan strategies to be effective. You run the risk of becoming just a glorified fire extinguisher if your main focus is problem solving. As well, you might be developing clones, not freethinkers and innovative team members. You must go beyond solving problems to improving the performance that may be causing the problems. StaffCoaching™ is all about taking people to the next, higher level in their performance.

To illustrate: Fine-tuning your fuel injection won't necessarily win the Indy 500. But deciding to win the Indy will require improved fuel injection. Another example: Teaching your team conflict-resolution skills won't increase productivity. But giving them responsibility for increased productivity will demand conflict-resolution skills. You need both — but team accountability is all-important. Optimum results come from a unified, objective-oriented, growing team.

Summary

Integrating a team involves StaffCoaching™ techniques and the appropriate approach. Like individuals, teams require coaching, mentoring and counseling. The challenge you face is one of sheer numbers. Problems multiply when you deal with a team of people.

As a coach, distinguish between a group and a team. Teams share a common goal, and that is what gives you the optimum results you want. Integrating the talents and strengths of your people into a cohesive team gives them the accountability and the ability to exponentially expand their impact.

"Great minds have purposes. Others have wishes."
—Washington Irving

6

How you do this is through sharing a vision, involving the team, rewarding achievement.

What keeps managers from becoming real coaches is how they recognize and reward the team. You can raise your team's level of awareness of their potential and their ability by what you reward. You can impact their own interpersonal skills so that they have the ability and comfort level to recognize one another. You do this by consciously scheduling actions into your daily planner. Elicit the help of the team to achieve higher results. Harness the power of technology and make communications seamless and information available. Create a fun, celebratory atmosphere which increases enjoyment and buy-in. Develop individuals and create teams.

Chapter Quiz

1. What are the four steps to developing a vision for your team?

2. List three signals of employee unrest.

3. Before you respond to a team problem or difficulty, what are eight preparatory steps you should consider?

6

?

4. What are five ways you can make it easier for your team to prioritize and follow through on tasks?

5. What one thing in this chapter will mean most to your own team if you apply it this week?

CHAPTER 7

Managing Within the StaffCoaching™ Model

People seem to think that anybody can coach. If you can manage, you can coach. While it is questionable that everyone can manage, there is no doubt that not everyone can coach. Some people just don't get it. Knowing how to do something well and inspiring that performance in others require completely different skills, outlook and temperament. Managing within the StaffCoach™ Model facilitates that shift in orientation.

> *"Coaching isn't an addition to the manager's job, it's an integral part of it."*
>
> — George Odiorne

Doing or Developing

The most noticeable error made by managers in attempting to coach is trying to get the person or the team to do as they do. You will hear coaches extol their teams, "Do it like I'm showing you." At best, you achieve one of two results with this approach: You either create a miniature you, or you get short-term results. Miniature is an appropriate description because you'll never get exactly the same performance. A miniature you will give you diminutive results. And, that's if your people see, feel and hear exactly what and why you are doing whatever you're doing. Not having your background, knowledge and insights, how can they duplicate your actions?

> *Create opportunities for your team to shine.*

Managing within the StaffCoach™ Model means developing performance — your staff's potential to go

227

7

beyond what they are currently doing. This is invaluable in today's marketplace with exponential changes in technology and globalization providing cheaper, more skilled workers half the world away. Alternatives for getting results are increasingly feasible. Growing your human assets gives your associates and your organization negotiating power. Automation was the threat to business in the last century. Now, unskilled labor is the threat. Peter Drucker once commented that illiterate no longer meant not being able to read, but meant not reading. This equates with skilled employees today. Unskilled doesn't mean your staff is uneducated; it means they aren't getting the results you require. Managing by coaching, mentoring and counseling brings those skills to the forefront fast.

A Story About Managing

A manager set up a team to look at the way the department responded to customer requests and complaints. The team consisted of employees involved in various functions of customer service. The manager studied the way his team worked and decided that the average time to handle customer calls could be reduced from 72 to 24 hours by eliminating certain steps. At the first team meeting, he outlined the purpose and goal of the team, then presented his findings and asked the team to come up with a plan to reduce the turnaround time on requests and complaints.

The team responded by saying, "What do you need us for? It looks like you've done it all yourself."

Managing results is about getting commitment, everyone's commitment. Involving people at the end of a process isn't going to impact much on buy-in. In order to manage continued job performance, get the team involved fast and often. The extent of their contribution might rest on their experience and insight, which you can develop and facilitate. Start fast, do always and you are managing in a StaffCoaching™ way. To get to commitment, flex your approach in contributing, collaborating, communicating and challenging within each of the roles of the StaffCoach™.

Exercise

Consider the necessity of being flexible as a manager, alternating your approach as your people require it. There are 11 common reasons why even the best team members occasionally don't do what they're supposed to do. After each reason, you decide which of the StaffCoaching™ roles you would choose in order to respond best: coach, mentor or counselor.

As a review, in Chapter 3, the coaching role is defined as your approach to inspire and motivate team members who perform okay and who meet the standards of the task. You coach them for buy-in, to take that little bit more of an effort. The mentoring role, described in Chapter 4, is the instruction role — typically used for team members who perform above average. Guiding your top performers in career decisions and increasing their outlook add to their worth and the organization's future. The counseling role, covered in Chapter 5, is for confronting and correcting, and is used for members who perform below standard in one or more areas. Counseling is a managing tool for discipline as well as behavior change.

7

Situations

1. A team member doesn't know whether to do a certain task.

   _____

2. He doesn't know how to do it.

   _____

3. He thinks your way will not work.

   _____

4. He thinks his way is better.

   _____

5. He thinks something else is more important.

   _____

6. He sees no positive benefit for doing the task.

   _____

7. He thinks he is doing it right (but isn't).

   _____

8. He is rewarded for not doing it.

   _____

9. He is punished for doing it.

   _____

10. No negative consequences exist for poor attempts.

    _____

11. Obstacles exist that exceed his control.

    _____

Exercise Analysis

1. **Coach** — Motivate him to make decisions, take responsibility.

2. **Mentor** — Guide and instruct on how to find out, where to go, resources to use.

3. **Mentor and Counselor** — Provide insight as well as correction.

4. **Mentor or Counselor** — Instruct him how to do this and be open — his way may be better.

5. **Counselor** — Correct his understanding of priorities.

6. **Coach** — Inspire and motivate.

7. **Counselor** — Correct his performance, then move to coaching.

8. **Counselor and Coach** — Some people complain so often, managers get tired of it and give the job to someone else. The moment you do that, you reward negative behavior. State the expectations and manage the results.

9. **Mentor and Coach** — Some people never complain … they are always there. Consequently, they get the garbage jobs. Mentor these people with gratitude, and perhaps let them vent their feelings to you as a coach.

10. **Counselor** — Correct the situation, explaining what is happening.

11. **Coach then Mentor** — Show him what and why and how to deal with this.

Depending on how you read into the situations, you might choose a different approach than this author. The value of the exercise lies in the value of the StaffCoach™ Model: Base your flexibility on consistent decisions made by observing the level of performance.

Whenever you face problems with managing your team members or whenever you want to achieve more through your people, look to the StaffCoaching™ Model for guidance to the role that will best serve your purposes. Should you coach?

7

Mentor? Counsel? Identity the level of performance and what role you should play, and you will be able to manage results and achieve higher returns through your people.

Delegating and the StaffCoaching™ Role

If you are responsible for more than five to seven people, making team members into coaches and/or mentors is an important option for you. Having direct project responsibility for more than 10 people is very difficult. Studies done on collaboration and team effectiveness from such universities as Michigan, Duke, MIT, Stanford, and others all verify the others' findings: When you get to seven people, teamwork decreases and it becomes difficult to individually manage employees. Adding coaches or mentors from the team addresses this challenge. Multiplying (or delegating) is essential if you are going to be an effective StaffCoach™. To delegate coaching responsibilities successfully, you need to understand what to do before you delegate.

- First, tell the team member what you expect. Make sure he understands your expectations.

- Second, make sure the work has value. Give the person a sense of value for being picked to do the job.

- Finally, make the work "do-able." A great formula for making the work doable is the formula "V + E = M." It stands for Vision plus Enthusiasm equals Motivation.

Share your own vision (direction) for the task at hand, the possible approaches to it … the various project phases … the hoped-for result. Make the vision open-ended, inviting the team member to add to or modify your ideas, encouraging his ownership of the project.

Next, enthusiastically communicate the benefits of the project as they relate specifically to the team member(s). As you personalize project benefits in this manner, you add "destination" to the direction you've provided. And when direction and destination are present, they always result in motivation.

"I've never been in a game where there wasn't enough glory for everybody."

— Joe Paterno

7

If motivation is somehow absent from a project, you can generally find the reason for problems by analyzing the vision (direction) and enthusiasm (destination) you have communicated or failed to communicate.

Notice that while you may make a team member into a coach or mentor, you shouldn't make a team member into a counselor. Team members don't have the authority to confront or correct. That's your responsibility.

Exercise

Using the StaffCoaching™ Model, decide what each member needs in terms of the roles you will play in their professional lives. You'll respond to each of the following scenarios with one of five answers. Individuals will need to be 1) coached, 2) mentored or 3) counseled. By delegating, you have two additional options for managing. You may need to 4) make some members into coaches or 5) make some members into mentors.

Pretend for a moment that you recently accepted responsibility for taking a successful product prototype to production in only three months. You've been assigned a production crew. As the StaffCoach™, it's your job to get the most out of each team member in the very short time you have to develop the product.

Meet your production crew — seven people with very special talents and needs! Based on what you learn from the remarks of each, decide how each person should be managed.

Decide how to manage each of the following seven people in one of five ways.

1. You respond to the team member as coach.

2. You respond as mentor.

3. You respond as counselor.

4. Team member serves as an assistant coach.

5. Team member serves as a mentor.

> *"Partial commitment is dangerous."*
> — Tom Osborne

7

7

1. "Hi, I'm Jeff Henry. I have 10 years of manufacturing experience and took part in developing the product prototype we're now putting into production."

   I should use the following StaffCoaching™ role(s) in managing this person …

   _____

   because_____

   _____

2. "Hi. I'm Mike Smith. I'm really happy to have this job. I was recently hired specifically to work on this project."

   I should use the following StaffCoaching™ role(s) in managing this person …

   _____

   because_____

   _____

3. "Hello, I'm Mary Smith. You just met my husband. I am a supervisor on this project. I've been told that I have excellent communication skills and a great work record."

   I should use the following StaffCoaching™ role(s) in managing this person …

   _____

   because_____

   _____

4. "John Green here. All I want to say is that I'm going to be retiring soon."

   I should use the following StaffCoaching™ role(s) in managing this person ...

   _____

   because_____

   _____

5. "Hello. My name is Lee Chi. I don't speak English very good, but I work hard."

   I should use the following StaffCoaching™ role(s) in managing this person ...

   _____

   because_____

   _____

6. "My name is Jean Ehlers. I'm 21 years old and was hired about a year ago. I'm doing okay on my job, but I'm still very inexperienced as a machine operator."

   I should use the following StaffCoaching™ role(s) in managing this person ...

   _____

   because_____

   _____

7. "Jeri Sandberg here. I've been a design engineer with the company for five years. I can handle almost anything, except communicating with people ... and maybe getting to work on time."

   I should use the following StaffCoaching™ role(s) in managing this person ...

   _____

   because_____

   _____

7

Exercise Analysis

Delegating is not simply a management tool for getting more done with less. It is a means of developing your people. It's a necessary action within each approach of the StaffCoach™, depending upon timing and intent. How you decide to manage your team is based on how you read into the situation, their background and performance needs, and how you balance an individual's needs with that of the team. Compare your thoughts concerning the above exercise to the author's.

1. Jeff can benefit by mentoring. He is certainly an above-average team member. If you wrote that Jeff could also coach someone, you're probably right. But to let him take on that responsibility will also require your mentoring him. Set your expectations and how you will measure success. He will add much to the results of your team.

2. Mike may need your involvement in all three roles, but certainly as coach and mentor. Since a manager has the greatest impact on someone in the beginning hours and days of employment, you manage this person.

3. Mary is definitely a candidate for assistant mentor. The skills are there. The work record is there. You will also want to coach and mentor her so she feels confident as a mentor. With that help, Mary could probably also guide others, just as Jeff could.

4. Get the feeling that John's mind might be on other things? There may be a burnout factor here or an attitude of doing just enough to get by. You need to counsel and motivate him. If you do your job well, John's work experience could make him a great mentor or coach. Watch his performance and move quickly in your assessment of his performance level.

5. Much of your work culture could seem strange to Lee, but he brings hard work and determination to your team. What does Lee need? He needs to be coached — inspired and motivated: "You're doing great, Lee. Keep it up." — as he performs adequately. With his work ethic, you can harness motivation and responsibility. Counsel off-target

behaviors immediately. Lee may gradually need mentoring as well — maybe from Jeff or John.

6. Jean needs all the help you can give her — coaching, mentoring and counseling. The fact that she has been there a year and acknowledges that she is doing okay suggests that she thinks okay is good enough. Move her from okay to great.

7. Jeri needs counseling, doesn't she? You'll have to confront her in the counseling role about her tardiness. Then explain the importance of communications on a team. Clearly establish your expectations. When you are comfortable with her performance, you could consider someone … maybe Mary (in light of her leadership and project-management skills) … to mentor Jeri, especially in the area of communications. Once that's done, a good coach will look for ways to motivate her.

Personality and Your Coaching Role

Personality enters into everything you do as a coach. You lean toward roles in managing which fit with your personality, and have a tendency to avoid what isn't comfortable. That's normal human nature and marvelously explained by Maslow, Herzberg, McGregor or any other motivational expert. We do more of what makes us feel good and move away from what doesn't. A warm, outgoing personality may not have much fun with counseling. It's tough addressing people's weak areas and calling attention to things that must change. Likewise, a take-charge, directive personality will lean toward telling what to do, how to do it and when to do it. Involvement consists of let's watch you do what I tell you to do.

Whether you subscribe to the nature or nurture view of human behavior and personality, with regard to coaching, like managing, you put your preferences aside. Flexibility and adaptability are the values that are gold to the coach. They let you learn the behaviors that best meet the needs of the situation and the individual. Doing makes you less uncomfortable.

With regard to your team, managing is all about understanding the personality of your team, their tendencies and their preferences. Coaching is using that knowledge to shape and mold, grow and expand their behavior. By acknowledging their uniqueness, you grow trust and appreciation.

> *"You have a lot of skill in communicating clearly; you can use that to your advantage in this tough situation."*

> *"I have observed how you dislike speaking disrespectfully to someone. To be valuable in the meeting, you will need to address this."*

> *"Your directness has been an asset for correcting several flaws in the system. It can work against you with people. Try this."*

Knowledge, like involvement, gives you the means to motivate and encourage change. With rapport and connection, people will easily listen. StaffCoaching™ isn't about changing personality; it is about facilitating better results. You can coach behaviors that will let your associate adapt his personality to the task. Honoring and valuing the individual is demonstrated when you can appreciate his personality and ask for performance improvement.

Hurdles to Performing Your Coaching Role

In addition to staff size, multiple responsibilities and personality differences, knowing the attitudes and actions that can sabotage the best-laid managerial plans will increase your coaching skills. Certain approaches to coaching can be disastrous, as many well-intentioned managers have discovered too late.

Here are the eight most common errors in coaching that undermine managing the performance of any work team … however talented it or you may be!

1. Detached leadership

2. Lack of goals

3. Failure to provide perspective

4. Failure to be specific

5. Failure to secure commitment

6. Taking the course of least resistance

7. Failure to identify results

8. Impatience

Detached Leadership

Detached managers isolate themselves from their people. They seem to believe it's undignified to get too involved with team members. They tend to spend a lot of time alone in their offices. They communicate a "lonely-at-the-top" attitude — one that says it's not organizationally healthy to rub shoulders with the "common" people.

The truth is, nothing is more important than involvement and communication with the people you work with. Leadership expert Ken Blanchard summed it up this way: "The most successful managers spend 80 percent of their time with their people." Do you spend 80 percent of your time with members of your team? Or do you think, "How would I get my work done if I spent that much time with them?"

Consider this: If it's true that coaches exist to get results, not from themselves but from the people who work for them, where should you be spending most of your time? Remember also that everything starts at the top. Your attitude affects the people who work for you. That's why detached leadership can be such a problem. If you show no interest in or concern for your people, why should they give your goals or your standards a place of importance in their minds and hearts? They are your job.

Lack of Goals

If you lack goals, sooner or later you'll have serious coaching problems. You'll be like a ship without a rudder — going wherever the wind and waves take you.

7

Detached leaders spend a lot of time alone in their offices.

239

7

$$W$$
$$I$$
$$N$$

What are your team goals … short-range and long-range? Knowing them doesn't count if you can't articulate them. If you can't speak it or ink it, as motivational expert Denis Waitley says, you can't think it. Examples might include:

- Increase sales quotas by 10 percent one year from today.

- Schedule every team member for an Excel class.

- Turn over the budgeting process to each team supervisor.

- Implement a "You Are the Customer" service program next fall.

- Bring in outside training for handling conflict and criticism at work.

Can your team members list your goals? To win, every team needs to know What's Important Now (WIN). The key word in that formula is "now." For instance, have you ever stared at your "things to do" list and ended up doing nothing at all? The sheer volume of work absolutely blew you away! Everyone has experienced that. But then somehow each of us learns that to get all our tasks done, we simply have to tackle them one at a time. First things first. What's important now? Your team needs to know that. Only when you tell them the priorities will you see measurable progress.

In addition, the goals you and your team settle on must be:

- Consistent with organizational direction

    In other words, no team is an island. Apart from the organizational glue that holds you together, the team really has no professional reason for being. Therefore, make certain that your team goals line up with organizational directions. Don't set goals independent of the organizational structure (i.e., a three-day workweek), or you will be in for disappointments.

- Simple but exciting

    In order for your team goals to excite the team, you need team member input and ownership in each goal. That's why some very successful StaffCoaches™ have established team committees to brainstorm goals, submit team mission statements and develop a plan for measuring

Motivational goals must offer benefits your team views as worthy.

progress. Others have identified goals for their teams, but then turned them over to self-directed team committees to report regularly on progress toward achieving the goals.

In any case, exciting, motivational goals must offer benefits that your team views as worthy and real.

- In front of your people daily

  Some obvious ways to keep team goals in front of members daily are the following:

  1. Progress charts (updated daily)

  2. Team newsletters

  3. Daily "pump-up" coffee sessions

  4. Banners, buttons, posters ... even bumper stickers

  5. T-shirts

  6. Goals as the screen savers on network computers

Failure to Provide Perspective

Ever get assigned a task that didn't make sense to you? Ever tackle a job without having the slightest idea how it fit with anything ... how it worked within the "big picture"? You may have done it ... even done it well ... but it couldn't have been your best effort, or a really satisfying or rewarding one.

People don't give their best if they don't know why they do what they do. That's because they don't see their job as important. When you give them the "why" of their tasks, they can see its relevance — and the real job satisfaction can take place. This is critical for you as a coach to realize. This is a foundational piece for inspiring performance.

If you are like a majority of the managers in midsize to large American organizations, people work for you who don't understand what they contribute to the overall scheme of things. You should go to those people and say, "I'm sure you understand the importance of your job, but let me tell you how important I think it is." Then give them the "whys" of their job and how it works within the organization. Chances are good that they will take more pride and interest in what they're doing. They will begin to assume "ownership" of their performance. They will gradually become self-starters. They will have their own internal reasons for performing regardless of the external incentives offered!

Failure to Be Specific

You've seen this happen: A manager tells the team what he wants in broad terms. Then the manager is surprised when the result is not what he wanted. Or, the manager waits for somebody to start doing it. What happens when you wait for self-starters? You'll wait forever. Don't wait … motivate! Tell people … specific people … specifically what you expect of them.

Example

Coach:

You're right, Tom, your sales are down. Way down. What do you think the problem is?

Tom:

I honestly don't know. I'm doing all the things that used to work … making at least 30 calls a day … following up with company literature, networking for referrals. It's frustrating!

Coach:

Hmm. Might be time for something new.

Tom:

Like what?

Coach:

Well, you've been pretty active in church and scouting over the years, haven't you?

Tom:

Very active.

Coach:

That probably means you've come to understand the people in those settings … what they value and what they don't. You know what gets their attention.

> *If you aim at nothing, you can be sure that you will hit it!*

> *Don't wait … motivate!*

Tom:

If you're suggesting that I call people I know from church and scouting, I've done some of that ever since ...

Coach:

No, I'm suggesting something more. What if you put together a letter tailored to each of those markets, a letter that speaks to their values and needs ... positioning yourself as being uniquely able to understand them and meet those needs?

Tom:

Like I can give them a level of trust they can't get from others in my business?

Coach:

Right.

Tom:

What about the company brochure?

Coach:

Well, since it hasn't set the world on fire for you lately, why not try 20 or 30 letters without it? When you get appointments from phone follow-up, you can always give it to them then.

Tom:

You think this approach might work? I'm not really the best letter writer in the world.

Coach:

Do a couple of rough drafts by Monday and we'll work on polishing together. Sure, I think the idea has possibilities — and with you behind it, I think it has real potential!

Give your people goals, some ideas about how to accomplish them, a vote of confidence and a deadline. Redirect their thoughts if they don't sound or appear to be headed in the direction you think is better. Without clarity, individual responsibility or team commitment is ineffective.

7

> *"They conquer who believe they can."*
> — John Dryden

7

Failure to Secure Commitment

If no mutual commitment exists between the coach and the team, there isn't much of a team at all. You must have mutual commitment to goals. You can get it by spending time together. The more time you spend with someone, the better you can identify with his abilities and vision. You must spend time sharing goals, problems, victories and even fears. Mutual commitment develops only through time and effort. It all comes back to the "MBWA" principle mentioned earlier in this book — "Management by Walking Around"!

You may call what your team feels "commitment" and you may talk about the trust or the synergy. Abe Lincoln had a favorite puzzle that might clarify this hurdle for you: If you have a dog with four legs and a tail and you call the dog's tail a leg, how many legs does the dog have? Abe would laugh, reminding his listener that he could call it anything he wanted; it was still a tail.

Taking the Course of Least Resistance

If you settle for what you know is less than the best you or your people can deliver, you may avoid confrontation — you may even think you're "cutting your team some slack." But the reality is that you undermine not only your coaching credibility but also your team's long-term viability. When a team faces a tough opponent … win or lose … it comes out better than if it had faced some "no-contest" challenge.

Example

Coach:

Ken, I just finished reading through the copy you wrote for the Father's Day cards. Some neat stuff.

Ken:

Just "neat"? I was hoping for "splendid" or maybe even "dynamite."

Coach:

Well, it shows your talent. You couldn't hide that if you tried. But it's just not the "Ken quality" I always look forward to.

Ken:

What's wrong with it? The editor asked for 10 tries and I gave him 16!

Coach:

I noticed that. Editors always appreciate extras — but I also noticed in his requisition that he asked for some of that newer metric copy like you did during the fall season's brainstorm session last month.

Ken:

That stuff takes time, John. Maybe if he saw what I've done, he'd like it okay.

Coach:

He might. But doing that wouldn't line up with our team mission statement ... the part that says we will "meet and exceed requisitions with the best, most original material we can create." You wrote that, as I recall?

Ken:

Ouch!

Coach:

I think a couple more of those newer approaches would be all this assignment needs to be "dynamite," to use your word. And we're still two days away from the due date.

Ken:

Okay. I'll do it. But you're a hard man.

Coach:

Only because you've helped me recognize excellent copy-writing when I see it.

Notice how this confrontation doesn't focus as much on the project deficiency as it does on the coach's pride in and expectations of the employee? A coach always urges on his team to be the best it can be — and that occasionally calls for "corrective inspiration."

Don't ever hesitate to ask your team for its best. When they give it, they'll always be glad they did!

7

> *Don't ever hesitate to ask your team members for their best.*

Failure to Identify Results

> *When you accomplish a task, let your people know.*

The seventh block to coaching success is having no clear sense of results. If the people on your team don't feel like they're getting results, they will gradually lose motivation. When you accomplish a task or a goal, let your people know.

Many coaches have found that "Project Recaps" are helpful in ensuring this vital finishing touch in any team effort. Project recaps can take many forms, written or verbal. But however you choose to acknowledge team achievement, recapping a project should include at least seven points, as shown in the sample form here.

Project Recap

1. What was the original project goal?

   To pave six miles of cracked interstate highway.

2. What made it difficult and/or important?

   Unseasonably hot spring weather made it hard. The approaching summer vacation traffic made it urgent.

3. Who worked on the project?

   Three five-member crews headed by Pat, Roy and Terry.

4. What made the person(s) right for the task? (Be specific.)

   Their record for meeting repair deadlines are the best in the Highway Department.

5. What were the good aspects of the project? (Pinpoint individual effort.)

   Roy's jackhammer team worked overtime four days in a row. Terry's grader driver discovered a good new technique for preventing crumbling shoulders.

6. What problems called for solutions in progress?

   Pat's crew had to pump concrete at night to fill three eroded or collapsed sections.

7. What aspects of this project make you as coach proud of the team?

   It was the fastest time ever recorded for paving so much highway.

You could use this example as your speaking outline in a team meeting or as an outline for an e-mail to each team member. In any case, project recaps are simple but powerful team motivators. It's vitally important for team members to see results. Seeing is motivating; keeping something visible keeps it in the forefront of thinking. There are few things as satisfying as being able to say, "We did that! I had a part in making it happen!"

Impatience

To succeed as a coach, you must develop patience. It is one of the values critical to the effective coach. When you have explained something to someone 10 times and the person asks you to repeat it just one more time, you smile and repeat it once again. When your team suffers setbacks or doesn't reach goals as quickly as you would like, you smile, help your people pick themselves up and go at it again. You tell your team members over and over that you believe in them ... that you know they can do it. Walk your talk and then they will gradually begin to have patience with themselves!

The way that works is not at all complicated. The fact is, people fail. When they do, they will either 1) lose patience with themselves and quit or pout or both, or they will 2) understand that failure doesn't diminish them in your eyes and try again!

As you model patience for your team, they will begin to understand that your patience is more than a comforting character attribute. It's a response to reality — a response to your team's humanity. That growing, subconscious awareness supports your team to try anything once — but, more importantly, to try anything again!

7

Exercise

There are spaces provided below under the eight errors in coaching that were discussed on the previous pages. Write what you think are the opposite, positive qualities of each error (i.e., the opposite of "Detached Leadership" might be "Involved Leadership"). Then briefly describe how each positive quality could be applied right now in your own team environment.

7

1. **Detached Leadership**
   The opposite of this might be _____.
   How would my team benefit immediately if I applied this coaching quality?
   _____
   _____
   _____

2. **Lack of Goals**
   The opposite of this might be _____.
   How would my team benefit immediately if I applied this coaching quality?
   _____
   _____
   _____

3. **Failure to Provide Perspective**
   The opposite of this might be _____.
   How would my team benefit immediately if I applied this coaching quality?
   _____
   _____
   _____

4. **Failure to Be Specific**
   The opposite of this might be _____.
   How would my team benefit immediately if I applied this coaching quality?
   _____
   _____
   _____

5. Failure to Secure Commitment

The opposite of this might be _____.

How would my team benefit immediately if I applied this coaching quality?

_____

_____

_____

6. Taking the Course of Least Resistance

The opposite of this might be _____.

How would my team benefit immediately if I applied this coaching quality?

_____

_____

_____

7. Failure to Identify Results

The opposite of this might be _____.

How would my team benefit immediately if I applied this coaching quality?

_____

_____

_____

8. Impatience

The opposite of this might be _____.

How would my team benefit immediately if I applied this coaching quality?

_____

_____

_____

7

Four Points for Managing Within the StaffCoach™ Model

There are four important points to consider when you manage within the StaffCoaching™ process. These are the four "P's" on which the entire StaffCoaching™ philosophy stands or falls — four steps in preparing for the inevitable resistance, objections and complaints you will regularly face.

These points relate to each approach — coaching, mentoring, counseling.

1. **Plan.** You have to have a plan. Not to have a plan is to have a plan to fail!

2. **Practice.** You have to practice your plan. Practice and practice until it becomes a part of you.

3. **Patience.** You must have patience. Patience will help you to not react but act.

4. **Persistence.** Don't give up. Don't quit. Hang in there. Persistence will prevail!

The four "P's" are a great emergency outline for any action plan ... a great guideline for any managerial dilemma ... a great worksheet for thinking through a goal or objective. The four "P's" are powerful ... plain and simple. To illustrate, let's use the four "P's" as the StaffCoaching™ formula for managing team member complaints.

1. You should plan for the inevitable. Complaints shouldn't come as a surprise to you as a successful coach. You should expect resistance, objections and gripes and be ready for them. Every assignment, project or procedure has the potential to generate such opposition. If you haven't planned for opposition by imagining what it might be ... and what your responses will be ... you'd better start.

2. Once you know what you're going to say in response to resistance, you should practice those responses. Write down your responses ... say them out loud (in front of a mirror, if you like) ... but practice so you'll be entirely comfortable with your thinking and delivery.

True wisdom is like a river; the deeper it is, the less noise it makes.

7

250

3. After you know what you're going to say and have practiced it, then prepare to have patience when people finally do exhibit resistance in any form. (HINT: Your preparation up to this point will make having patience a lot easier!)

4. And, finally, you should use persistence in getting your point across. Don't imagine that every complainer will instantly buy in to your rationale just because you're the boss. If you believe your rationale, you'll stick to it — and then your team will believe it, too.

"If you think you can win, you can win."

— William Hazlitt

7

Exercise: Applying the Four "P's"

If the four "P's" work at all, they must work for you. So let's put them to the test. This exercise is designed to prepare you for your next major StaffCoaching™ challenge. You probably already know what that challenge is — or at least what it's likely to be.

In the box below, list the top three job situations that you dread. One such situation you dislike might be announcing a project everyone hates. Another could be dealing decisively with ongoing, inappropriate behavior from an individual or the group. After you have noted three such challenges, pick that one situation you feel least able to control. Fill in an approach to each of the four "P's" listed below.

a. _____

b. _____

c. _____

1. What PLAN can I think of that might make the situation as painless as possible? (It's always good to have an alternate plan, too.)

   _____

   _____

2. What specific PRACTICE would best prepare me for the upcoming encounter or occurrence? (Working through a speech? Arming myself with research or data?)

   _____

   _____

3. How is my PATIENCE likely to be tested? How can I be ready for the impatience I will undoubtedly feel? How will I counter it?

   _____

   _____

4. How will I demonstrate PERSISTENCE in presenting my plan or position? What responses to hypothetical resistance or complaints can I arm myself with?

   _____

   _____

Exercise Analysis

Considering the original definition of management — plan, organize, staff, direct, control — the four "P's" set up your StaffCoaching™ management for success. When you weave your values through each action, you can positively change any intervention.

Five Ways to Quiet Complaints

Managing is about changing behaviors to get results. Resistance is a normal reaction anytime you "manipulate" people. Managing that resistance is easy when you use the same principles as that of counseling. Focus on the specific resistance to a specific task, not the person. You can generally turn complaints around when people understand where you are coming from. There are five things you can tell them.

1. **Tell them why the job is important.** You read earlier about the need for job meaning. It is one of the top three reasons why people don't do what they are supposed to do. Once team members understand the importance of their jobs and how they contribute to the overall picture, their attitudes often change dramatically. You add value to them as people. To help make sure that you avoid complaints by adequately communicating job importance, complete these three statements before addressing your team.

    *   This job will benefit the organization because

        _____ .

    *   This project will benefit every team member because

        _____ .

    *   Failing to do this job well (or at all) will result in these long-term negative circumstances:

        _____ .

253

2. **Tell them what the desired results are.** When people don't know your specific expectations, they don't know where they're going, when the job will end, and whether or not they've done a good job. Being kept in the dark is very demoralizing. Always define desired results, and watch people respond positively. Here are five key questions your team will need to know to be motivated by the results you seek.

   - How will the results be achieved as a team? By individual team members?

   - Are the results one time or ongoing? Explain.

   - How will the team know when the desired results are accomplished?

   - What team rewards are associated with the desired results?

   - What factors must be overcome to achieve the desired results (time constraints, equipment limitations, etc.)?

3. **Assign and define job authority.** If you give a team member responsibility for an aspect of a project, you must support him by also giving him the authority to make it happen. Other team members must know this person has the authority. There are two basic ways to publicize who's in charge: by written assertion or by personal announcement to the members concerned. In either approach, you must answer the following three questions to everyone's satisfaction to make sure the authority "sticks" that you're about to transfer.

   - How will the authority be used on a daily basis?

   - Exactly how are team members expected to respond?

   - What are the benefits of responding to this new authority — and what are the consequences of failing to respond?

   If you want to develop a potential leader and maximize the chances of project success, let the person have the authority to do the job … not just the responsibility. Notice how the three questions above use each approach

Problems are those things people see when they take their eyes off the goal.

of the StaffCoach™. You mentor to clarify importance, you coach for clarity and you counsel for accountability.

4. **Agree on deadlines.** Be careful with assumptions. When you give an assignment, people won't automatically know when it's due. Spell out deadlines clearly. Leaving something to chance will add to your stress and unnecessarily risk your results. To make sure deadlines are M.E.T., you should …

Monitor milestones.

Build in periodic progress checks before the project completion date.

Energize efforts.

If project phases are lagging, suggest ideas and/or change procedures or personnel to bring the project back up to speed.

Trumpet the team!

Did you meet the deadline? Find some way to celebrate it. The celebration doesn't have to be a big deal — a quick meeting to acknowledge key players, an inexpensive lunch at a favorite "out of office" gathering place, going to the individuals and thanking them. Recognize the effort. The important thing is this: Don't let a deadline victory slip by without a "trumpeting the team" celebration.

5. **Provide feedback.** Ask your staff to give you feedback, written or spoken, on how the job is going. How could it have been planned better? How do team members feel you have responded to their needs? The act of seeking ideas and opinions through open-ended questions will boost the morale of your team more than the greatest pep talk ever spoken!

The road to success is marked with tempting parking places.

Feedback is an interesting management and communication tool. Managers will acknowledge that they want it and need it. They will seek out their bosses, check with their clients or observe their people to determine how they are doing. The breakfast of champions. Yet, they aren't as regular and consistent in giving it. Managing results means continually giving feedback. It is feedback that energizes and propels action.

Team Collaboration

Collaboration is an interesting word when considering management. It is a tool for the coach, but is it a result of management or an action? Collaboration isn't communication or cooperation. It is a higher level skill built around the values noted in Chapter 1. For the StaffCoach™, it is a result which leads to a greater result.

To improve performance, motivation and buy-in, trust and respect are necessary for long-term successes. Collaborating and communicating synergistically make the results-focus of your management even more meaningful. The quicker you can bring your team's skills to the level where they can collaborate, the quicker you increase outcomes.

If team decisions are based on the arbitrary opinion of your management or that of the loudest and most forceful team member, you can expect only minimum support and even less enthusiasm from the team in implementing them. The joint discussion and decision making generated by collaboration respect each member's insights and give you the opportunity to capitalize on all the combined strengths. This builds in the necessary flexibility to accommodate special circumstances that can arise. When your team is collaborating on performance, they are setting up that performance for optimum results.

Loss of self-esteem is built on failure. It's no fun missing a deadline, messing up a project or causing your team to mishandle a customer. When you have harnessed the energy of the team in achieving results, their collaborative effort is much stronger than any one member. When there is failure, there is discussion, planning and support. Collaboration raises the esteem level of individuals and their group. With collaboration as your goal, team members will buy in to the team's accountabilities.

Summary

Once your team sees that what they do makes a difference to the organization and is valued by you, they will perform at higher levels. Managing within the StaffCoach™ Model ensures that. Performance Coach Gail Cohen notes that success evolves from understanding the correct order of have-do-be: I have this and do this and thus am who I am. Your coaching elicits their innate strengths, your mentoring increases their abilities to do, and your counseling shapes who they can be. By managing through developing people, delegating accountability, overcoming hurdles and dealing with complaints, you become a motivator for increased results.

Your employees need you more than a pay raise. When you manage through providing personal thanks, making time for your team, and giving them consistent and constant feedback, you energize them for the increased pressures and challenges that are a reality in today's workplace.

Creating an open environment through M.E.T. and continually keeping associates clear on the why, what and how of their individual and joint responsibilities add to job satisfaction. You handle the stressors and frustrations that occur through supplying information, involving your people and rewarding performance. By doing these StaffCoaching™ actions, your management develops a sense of ownership and gives each associate a chance to grow and learn. Those are actions to celebrate. Celebrating success is the action you take to perpetuate the coaching cycle.

StaffCoaching™ is managing as a motivator. It recognizes that your results do come through your people.

7

7

Chapter Quiz

1. Explain the V + E = M formula for making a team project "do-able."

   V _____

   E _____

   M_____

2. What are the four "P's" that prepare the StaffCoach™ for leadership resistance?

   _____

   _____

   _____

3. Name three of the five elements necessary to overcome project objections and/or complaints.

   _____

   _____

   _____

4. List the five questions that need answers in order to motivate a team to complete a project.

   _____

   _____

   _____

5. What is the significance of M.E.T.?

   M_____

   E _____

   T _____

CHAPTER 8

So What and Who Cares!

An old management adage is *act as if.* This suggests that if you do something and keep doing it, soon you will become successful at it. In terms of self-confidence, the belief is that acting as if you were confident will eventually result in you being confident.

StaffCoaching™ is a never-ending process. Once you achieve new levels of performance, those levels become the new standard. You start the process all over again. As your people grow and succeed, they, in turn, regenerate the process. Achievement builds trust, trust builds respect. There is more communication, people honor each other, disagreement is a means of innovation — and the process goes on.

There is no one right way, no specific order to perform your StaffCoaching™ roles. You begin where performance dictates, coach with your associate or the team, or as a mentor or counselor. You use the role you need at that moment to match the problem. This manual has given you a model and a series of guides to facilitate and strengthen your own judgment.

Teamwork is a journey, not a destination.

The Coach Attitude

We began this book by identifying those values which successful coaches embody. Coaches imprint their values on the people who are on their team. Inherent in each value is a positive attitude. An important responsibility of yours as the StaffCoach™ is to exhibit a positive attitude. Your attitude translates those values into team activity that supports company objectives. You project and transfer these positive values through specific actions.

1. Setting an example

2. Being fair and equitable

3. Seeking the participation and involvement of each team member

4. Honoring each member of your team

Exercise

Following are three scenarios. Each one reflects one of the three ways of projecting a positive StaffCoach™ philosophy. Each scenario is done first the "right way" and then the "wrong way." See if you can spot the StaffCoach™ techniques that aren't implemented … as well as those that are implemented in projecting a positive philosophy to team members.

1. Setting an Example

The Right Way

Coach:

Well, let's take a break and pick back up in about 10 minutes, okay?

(As all leave but Jenny) *I think we're getting some good ideas for this new project, don't you?*

Jenny:

Yes. No thanks to Nancy.

Coach:

What do you mean?

Jenny:

Nothing she's said has been new. They're the same ideas we heard and rejected last time we had a brainstorm session.

Coach:

I like her open sharing. I think some of her thoughts have potential.

Jenny:

Give me a break.

Coach:

Jenny, because an idea wasn't quite right for one project doesn't mean it couldn't work for another. New is relative.

Jenny:

If you say so.

Coach:

Relax and enjoy the session. Or better yet, try to think of something you could add to ideas you don't like that could make them better. You're good at things like that, just like Nancy is good at telephone sales.

Exercise Analysis

What did the StaffCoach™ do right?

_____

_____

What would you have done differently? Why?

_____

_____

What should StaffCoach™ follow-up be as a result of this scenario?

_____

_____

The Wrong Way

Coach:

Well, let's take a break and pick back up in about 10 minutes, okay?

(As all leave but Jenny) I think we're getting some good ideas for this new project, don't you?

Jenny:

Yes. No thanks to Nancy.

Coach:

Well, everybody has bad days once in a while.

Jenny:

Bad? Nothing she's said has been new. They're the same ideas we heard and rejected last time we had a brainstorm session.

Coach:

Yeah. We've got to be patient with her. Besides, we're making good progress in spite of her. Let's just let her talk once in a while and hope we keep getting good ideas from the rest of us.

Exercise Analysis

What did the StaffCoach™ do wrong?

_____

_____

What would you have done differently? Why?

_____

_____

What should StaffCoach™ follow-up be as a result of this scenario?

_____

_____

2. **Being Fair and Equitable**

   The Right Way

   Jean:

   Claire, Rita just told me someone would probably have to visit the Dallas client next weekend. Is that true?

   Claire:

   Yes. I just heard about it an hour ago myself.

   Jean:

   Well, I know it's my turn to go, but my sister and her family are going to be in town that weekend. Can you please get someone else to do it?

   Claire:

   I can ask if someone would like to trade with you and ...

   Jean:

   No one will! Everybody hates that client.

   Claire:

   That sounds like one huge generalization.

   Jean:

   Why don't you send the new girl? She hasn't been assigned a spot on the travel roster yet. She'd probably consider it an honor.

Claire:

No, I don't think that would be good. I want her to travel with someone else a few times until she learns the ropes. But I'll tell you what I will do.

Jean:

What?

Claire:

If nobody will trade with you, I think I could probably go to Dallas that weekend.

Exercise Analysis

What did Claire do right?

_____

_____

What would you have done differently? Why?

_____

_____

What should StaffCoach™ follow-up be as a result of this scenario?

_____

_____

The Wrong Way

Jean:

Claire, Rita just told me someone would probably have to visit the Dallas client next weekend. Is that true?

Claire:

Yes. I just heard about it an hour ago myself.

Jean:

Well, I know it's my turn to go, but my sister and her family are going to be in town that weekend. Can you please get someone else to do it?

Claire:

I can ask if someone would like to trade with you and ...

Jean:

No one will! Everybody hates that client. Why don't you send the new girl? She hasn't been assigned a spot on the travel roster yet.

Claire:

I don't know. That could be a little like throwing a sheep to the wolves.

Jean:

Or it could be the best thing that's ever happened. She's a Mexican-American and the client is, too. It might end up being the perfect match.

Claire:

Umm. Well, okay. But this is just between you and me—and if we lose a promising new girl because of this, it will be your job to find a new one.

Exercise Analysis

What did Claire do wrong?

_____

_____

What would you have done differently? Why?

_____

_____

What should StaffCoach™ follow-up be as a result of this scenario?

_____

_____

3. **Seeking Participation and Involvement**
   The Right Way

Barb:

So how much computer equipment is missing?

Joan:

About $6,000 worth. Two units and a hard disk.

Barb:

Any ideas about how it happened?

Joan:

None. Except I know it wasn't anyone on the team. Ever since you gave us the key to the equipment room, each of us has taken turns with hourly inventory.

Barb:

What does security say about it?

Joan:

That it was probably an inside job. But I still say that it wasn't one of the team, Barb. No one would betray the trust the company gave us by giving us access to that room.

Barb:

I believe that, too. I certainly have no reason to think otherwise.

Joan:

But you probably want the key back, right?

Barb:

No. I want your team to work out a system with security that makes it impossible for someone to get out of here with $6,000 worth of equipment. And one more thing.

Joan:

What's that?

Barb:

Tell the team I really like the increased figures I saw last week.

Exercise Analysis

What did Barb do right?

_____

_____

What would you have done differently? Why?

_____

_____

What should StaffCoach™ follow-up be as a result of this scenario?

_____

_____

The Wrong Way

Barb:

So how much computer equipment is missing?

Joan:

About $6,000 worth. Two units and a hard disk.

Barb:

Any ideas about how it happened?

Joan:

None. Except I know it wasn't anyone on the team. Ever since you gave us the key to the equipment room, each of us has taken turns with hourly inventory.

Barb:

Well, I'm afraid I'm going to need that key back, anyway … at least until we can prove it was no one on the team.

Joan:

I wish you wouldn't, Barb. It will look like you suspect everyone.

Barb:

Maybe. But I can't risk another theft while we're investigating the first one. Upper management would think I was crazy!

Exercise Analysis

What did Barb do wrong?

_____

_____

What would you have done differently? Why?

_____

_____

What should StaffCoach™ follow-up be as a result of this scenario?

_____

_____

Attitude and Values

The StaffCoaching™ Model focuses your attention on the constant imprinting of values. If someone is turning in a performance that is above standard, you communicate specific values through the role of a mentor. If it's standard performance, those values come through in your coaching. If it's substandard, you honor and respect the associate through your counseling. To be effective, you demonstrate the values of flexibility and sensitivity to the needs of your people.

Betty Eadie wrote in *Handbook for the Heart*, "The more you notice the love, the miracles, and the beauty around you, the more love comes into your life. The more you love, the greater your ability to love. And the process perpetuates itself." This is the real reward for mastering the values of the StaffCoach™. The more you value your people, supporting them, energizing them, guiding and encouraging them, the more you honor them. They in turn respect, appreciate and act on your direction and advice. The process perpetuates itself.

When employees are asked who made an impact on them and what caused that impact, specific values and attitudes are addressed. From these comments, an encouraging, influential manager can be summarized as one who:

- Listens to you, really listens.
- Respects your abilities, believes in you.
- Sees what you do right as well as pointing out what you do wrong.
- Can delegate responsibility.
- Has enthusiasm.
- Has a sense of humor.
- Admits mistakes herself.
- Gives you credit for your ideas.
- Recognizes when you need a lift and is there.
- Is interested in you as a person.
- Is at peace with herself.

8

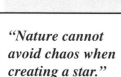

- Has consistent rules and has the staff play a part in developing those rules.

- Is a good teacher, willing to share ideas.

- Criticizes constructively.

- Follows through on promises.

- Is honest, genuine, real.

The Key Ingredients

The StaffCoaching™ skills that encourage performance improvement are sustained by continuous assessment of results and constant adjustments in your approach. As your people contribute and as successes increase in terms of improvement, you know your approach is right. This dynamic process requires you to be adept at change. Knowledge of your options strengthens your ability to see change as a positive.

Keep your focus on what your people need to improve and to support their own development. Your associates require seven specific things from your coaching. Each in turn demands actions by you to take them to that next level of performance. To review, your people benefit from these basic ingredients for obtaining results.

1. **A basic understanding of your expectations concerning their jobs.**

    You enable this by:

    - Developing with them clarity on what their jobs, their roles, their responsibilities, necessary relationships and required results are.

    - Involving them in goal setting.

    - Agreeing to measurements to track their performance.

2. **A continued awareness of what is expected of individuals and their integration within the team.**

   You enable this by:

   - Keeping your people aware of organizational goals, vision, mission, changes and needs.

   - Creating understanding about the importance and contribution of each team member and the team in regard to the organization and change.

   - Working with the team members as changes in priority necessitate a change in plans, implementation or organization of work.

3. **The opportunity and necessity of involvement in planning performance strategies and in decision making.**

   You enable this by:

   - Encouraging and implementing associates' ideas.

   - Rewarding involvement and risk taking.

   - Delegating the roles and responsibilities of the StaffCoach™.

4. **Continuous and constant support, direction and encouragement.**

   You enable this by:

   - Encouraging their questions and points of disagreement.

   - Providing guidance or correction when problems occur.

   - Leading them to resources and to awareness about additional considerations.

5. **Regular feedback on performance before, during and after tasks.**

   You enable this by:

   - Frequently reviewing results in relation to each action and the goals, as projects go on.

8

- Openly and honestly letting associates know what they are doing in relation to their own performance and the team.

- Discussing performance in terms of their potential.

6. **Recognize and reward performance based on individual improvements.**

You enable this by:

- Expressing appreciation for the work and the team member.

- Calling attention, privately and publicly, to improvements.

- Celebrating accomplishments.

7. **Establish a work environment that respects and facilitates individual responsibility and self-growth.**

You enable this by:

- Establishing relationships with team members that honor them as capable and talented individuals.

- Underscoring their strengths and achievements.

- Sharing insights, success stories and resources.

Notice how each ingredient emphasizes one approach more than another within the StaffCoach™ Model. Coaching sets expectations, mentoring furthers understanding, counseling sets or resets direction. All three roles involve, give feedback, reward and encourage self-development. High-performing teams are interactive and interdependent; these basic ingredients of StaffCoaching™ minimize the frictions and challenges.

Tools for Your Team

StaffCoaching™ gives your associates innumerable tools. Consider: Your purpose is to improve performance in order to get results for your organization. You get those results through coaching, mentoring and counseling your people to achieve greater performance. By adapting your approaches of supporting and encouraging, energizing and instructing, guiding and correcting, you give your people real tools for their own self-management.

- **The ability to make choices**

  Coaching teaches people that the choices they make cause the outcomes they get. Supporting them encourages their own analysis of what and how to do things.

- **Taking risks and trying new ways**

  Pushing people to higher performance levels necessitates that they move out of their comfort zones. Success can breed stagnation, and habit can initiate fear in trying different methods.

- **Self-analysis**

  Encouraging performance change and asking for associates' opinions on how to do this facilitates reflecting on their own strengths and thought processes. Insights into their own behavior give them the energy and courage to change.

- **Self-awareness**

  There are often huge gaps between what people think they do and what they actually do. Your feedback, honesty and sharing of information can help associates understand what they do and say and the impact they have on other team members.

- **The need for practice**

  Counseling better ways to do a job requires practice in order to achieve mastery. By insisting on practice and improvement, you give your people the discipline to continue building on skills and not accepting the status quo.

- **Personal commitment**

  As you reward and celebrate team communication and collaboration, you facilitate a sense of commitment in your team members. Nobody will commit to losing. Your associates realize a sense of commitment by the results and achievements, the vision and security you provide.

8

8

- **The ability to collaborate**

  Talking is usually at someone rather than with someone. Teaching your people how to dialogue — talk with — gives them an ability to collaborate. Rewarding team successes strengthens their appreciation of consensus. They better understand that either they win together, or it isn't a win.

What's in it for them, your people, is intertwined in what's in it for you. Achieving results through your people gives them the same tools that give you successes. Few people who have achieved real acclaim can say they did it alone. Someone helped them help themselves. Your actions may be so subtle, so well orchestrated, that your people are unaware or unappreciative of the time. Regardless, you have a very positive impact. Your people develop real job skills and career skills that will benefit them on the job, at home, in their community endeavors, and with their personal interests.

The Wisdom of Coaching

Joe Gilliam, a leading author and corporate coach, notes that StaffCoaching™ isn't about a best leadership style or about MBO (Management By Objectives). Both are important. Coaching, however, is about serving. The qualities of the StaffCoach™ can be summarized by three words: permission, protection and process.

Giving your people permission to try harder, grow and stretch, supports them and builds self-esteem. Your responsibility concerning protection reminds you that achievements and recognition belong to the team. You take accountability for the failures. The process is ever-changing as you coach and mentor and counsel.

When your team realizes that you do give them permission, will protect their integrity and are there for them, trust and collaboration bring about synergy. Your people grow, develop and succeed in three ways, including:

1. Trial and error, pain and suffering
2. Finding someone successful and copying what they do
3. Benefiting from your coaching, mentoring and counseling

Watching you, listening to you and doing what you direct grow performance. Your team watches and listens because of the support and acceptance that permeate everything you do with and for your team.

Exercise

An exercise to increase your own wisdom as well as your impact on your people centers around appreciating your people as your most valuable assets.

1. Think about the number of accomplishments that your associates achieved in the last month. These can be small or large, individual or team. Consider a number that represents the amount of accomplishments or results they caused.

2. Now, count the amount of times you recognized, acknowledged or rewarded accomplishments and achievements of your people.

3. Compare those two numbers.

Exercise Analysis

Rarely do the numbers match. The opportunities for recognizing accomplishments seldom equal the amount of times a coach tells her people how great, successful and skilled they are. On average, a good coach acknowledges performance improvement one out of every four times.

So what? Who cares? You better. The whole StaffCoach™ Model is based on performance-management techniques and behavior modification. You get what you reward. Focus on recognition of a behavior and you will get more of that behavior. Coach positively, communicate positively, reward positively. Your people care. Your organization benefits.

Nonperformance occurs not because of a flaw on your people's part. Certainly they do or don't do something that gives you poor results or lesser performance than you require. But whose fault is that? The premise of this manual makes that clear: You cause, encourage, set up results. Employee or team non-performance occurs because of your poor coaching. StaffCoaching™ is about the interventions you take to build performance improvement. The old upper-management challenge, "That's what you did yesterday; what are you going to do for me today?" turns into a positive IF you recognize yesterday's successes and build on those achievements. Continuous improvement is possible with coaching wisdom and consistency.

Lasting Impact

Your most important impact as a manager and coach centers on your people — what they do. A significant role of coaching is creating the work environment that allows employees to be motivated. All associates want to be magnificent. You facilitate their ability to excel by supporting and instructing and guiding.

Encourage your people to find balance in their lives and model how. Enthusiasm and celebration will allow this. One wise coach provided her people with these guiding words:

- Take time for work; it is the price of success.

- Take time to think; it is the source of power.

- Take time to play; it is the secret of youth.

- Take time to read; it is the foundation of wisdom.

- Take time to be friendly; it is the road to happiness.

- Take time to dream; it's hitching your wagon to a star.

- Take time to love; it is the highest joy of life.

- Take time to laugh; it is the music of the soul.

Give your people the resources and support to be magnificent. Give them permission and protection. A story about Pablo Picasso illustrates how you can have lasting impact. When a patron asked him what she could do to support the painter's success, Picasso responded, "Get out of my light."

You are at your best when you give your associates your time, your insights, your encouragement and enthusiasm, and then step out of the way.

The rules for success keep changing, but success stays centered. You succeed in having an impact by realizing that your ideas and your knowledge aren't enough. Serve your people's fundamental needs for recognition and appreciation. Relentlessly push your team to improve. Value their performance.

Consider this: If Mozart and Paul McCartney traded places in history, would Mozart become the greatest rock star of our time? Would McCartney have been the greatest composer of that era? Both had prodigious work ethics, spectacular dexterity, compelling ambition, and the charisma to charm royal audiences as well as common laborers. How about Jack Welch and Mother Teresa? Both had a passionate vision, strong beliefs, a crowd of zealous followers. Would they be as successful if they found themselves in each other's shoes?

The answer is "yes" for the same reason that you will succeed in whatever industry or career you choose. The inherent qualities that make artists great, leaders outstanding and coaches excel are relevant and unchanging regardless of time or audience. Those qualities are respect for your people, flexibility, communication,

8

singular vision, and unwavering focus on results. When your purpose is outward, on your people, your impact is lasting.

In *Chicken Soup for the Soul*, the authors went back to 1100 A.D. for words of wisdom. It serves as a fitting conclusion to your importance as a coach and your reason for being: modeling performance improvement. We have so many lofty goals and aspirations. We look outward to what we can do. It's easy to overlook the answer: a continuous act of becoming.

"When I was young and free and my imagination had no limits, I dreamed of changing the world. As I grew older and wiser, I discovered the world would not change, so I shortened my sights somewhat and decided to change only my country.

"But it, too, seemed immovable.

"As I grew into my twilight years, in one last desperate attempt, I settled for changing only my family, those closest to me, but alas, they would have none of it.

"And now as I lie on my deathbed, I suddenly realize: If I had only changed myself first, then by example I would have changed my family.

"From my inspiration and encouragement, I would then have been able to better my country and, who knows, I may have even changed the world."

INDEX

Taking Aim on Leadership

And Making Success Your Target
by Peter Capezio and Debra Morehouse

Item # 5401 $26.95

Do you demonstrate real leadership ability? Do you influence the way people think, feel and act? Energize your leadership style and create success! Hit the bull's-eye when you take AIM on leadership! Set the pace for high-quality, high-energy performance throughout your organization. Whether you are a business leader or an individual leader, this book is for you.

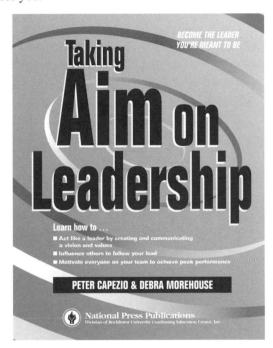

You'll Learn How to:

- Build your leadership competence at every level

- Create teams that can respond quickly, accurately and with exceptional quality

- Apply the right leadership style at the right time

- Develop a model for leadership success that everyone can buy into

- Increase the morale and performance of others

- Forge dynamic links between individual and team goals — links that will inspire everyone to a higher performance

- Empower others by unleashing their potential to meet the challenges of the global market

- Develop the skills that allow you to be a leader of tomorrow

- Take the necessary steps to achieve self-directed leadership

- Be perceived as a role model in all that you do!

Think Like a Manager

Everything they didn't tell you when they promoted you!
by Roger Fritz, Ph.D.

Item # 5413 $26.95

Few people are born with the skills to be effective in a management position. Those who succeed do so because they have committed themselves to the pursuit of excellence … to developing their skills as professional managers to the highest degree possible. This book not only tells you how you can do it, but it even shows you the way.

This interactive self-study manual presents a step-by-step, how-to strategy for building the skills every manager needs to be effective. This is not like every other management book. It's not about the newest fad or the latest hype. It is about the nuts and bolts of managing, of establishing and meeting objectives, of getting results through people and being measured by those results. It's about what you need to do to grow and prosper as a professional manager.

You'll Learn How to:

- Establish and meet realistic goals and objectives
- Develop skills in planning and time management
- Master the secrets of motivating yourself and your staff
- Give performance appraisals that increase productivity and improve staff morale
- Build teamwork and cooperation
- Solve the everyday problems and crises that all managers face

YOUR BACK-OF-THE-BOOK STORE

ORDER FORM

Because you already know the value of National Press Publications Desktop Handbooks and Business User's Manuals, here's a time-saving way to purchase more career-building resources from our convenient bookstore.

- IT'S EASY … Just make your selections, then visit us on the Web, mail, call or fax your order. (See back for details.)
- INCREASE YOUR EFFECTIVENESS … Books in these two series have sold more than two million copies and are known as reliable sources of instantly helpful information.
- THEY'RE CONVENIENT TO USE … Each handbook is durable, concise and filled with quality advice that will last you all the way to the boardroom.

60-MINUTE TRAINING SERIES™ HANDBOOKS

TITLE	ITEM #	RETAIL PRICE*	QTY.	TOTAL
8 Steps for Highly Effective Negotiations	#424	$14.95		
Assertiveness	#4422	$14.95		
Balancing Career and Family	#4152	$14.95		
Common Ground	#4122	$14.95		
The Essentials of Business Writing	#4310	$14.95		
Everyday Parenting Solutions	#4862	$14.95		
Exceptional Customer Service	#4882	$14.95		
Fear & Anger: Control Your Emotions	#4302	$14.95		
Fundamentals of Planning	#4301	$14.95		
Getting Things Done	#4112	$14.95		
How to Coach an Effective Team	#4308	$14.95		
How to De-Junk Your Life	#4306	$14.95		
How to Handle Conflict and Confrontation	#4952	$14.95		
How to Manage Your Boss	#493	$14.95		
How to Supervise People	#4102	$14.95		
How to Work With People	#4032	$14.95		
Inspire and Motivate: Performance Reviews	#4232	$14.95		
Listen Up: Hear What's Really Being Said	#4172	$14.95		
Motivation and Goal-Setting	#4962	$14.95		
A New Attitude	#4432	$14.95		
The New Dynamic Comm. Skills for Women	#4309	$14.95		
The Polished Professional	#4262	$14.95		
The Power of Innovative Thinking	#428	$14.95		
The Power of Self-Managed Teams	#4222	$14.95		
Powerful Communication Skills	#4132	$14.95		
Present With Confidence	#4612	$14.95		
The Secret to Developing Peak Performers	#4962	$14.95		
Self-Esteem: The Power to Be Your Best	#4642	$14.95		
Shortcuts to Organized Files and Records	#4307	$14.95		
The Stress Management Handbook	#4842	$14.95		
Supreme Teams: How to Make Teams Work	#4303	$14.95		
Thriving on Change	#4212	$14.95		
Women and Leadership	#4632	$14.95		

TITLE	RETAIL PRICE	QTY.	TOTAL
The Assertive Advantage #439	$26.95		
Being OK Just Isn't Enough #5407	$26.95		
Business Letters for Busy People #449	$26.95		
Dealing With Conflict and Anger #5402	$26.95		
Complete Guide to Finding and Hiring the Right People #54052	$26.95		
High-Impact Presentation and Training Skills #4382	$26.95		
Learn to Listen #446	$26.95		
The Manager's Role as Coach #456	$26.95		
The Memory System #452	$26.95		
Negaholics® No More #5406	$26.95		
Parenting the Other Chick's Eggs #5404	$26.95		
Taking AIM On Leadership #5401	$26.95		
Prioritize, Organize: Art of Getting It Done 2nd ed. #4532	$26.95		
The Promotable Woman #450	$26.95		
Think Like a Manager 3rd ed. #4513	$26.95		
Working Woman's Comm. Survival Guide #5172	$29.95		

SPECIAL OFFER:
Orders over $150.00 receive
FREE SHIPPING

Prices and availability subject to
change without notice.

Subtotal	$
Add 7% Sales Tax *(Or add appropriate state and local tax)*	$
Shipping and Handling *($6 one item; 50¢ each additional item)*	$
Total	$

VOLUME DISCOUNTS AVAILABLE — CALL 1-800-258-7248

Name_____Title_____

Organization _____

Address _____

City _____State/Province _____ZIP/Postal Code _____

Payment choices:

❑ Enclosed is my check/money order payable to National Seminars.

❑ Please charge to: ❑ MasterCard   ❑ VISA   ❑ American Express

Signature _____Exp. Date _____Card Number _____

❑ Purchase Order #_____

MAIL: Complete and mail order form
with payment to:
National Press Publications
P.O. Box 419107
Kansas City, MO 64141-6107

PHONE:
Call toll-free **1-800-258-7248**

FAX:
1-913-432-0824

INTERNET: www.NationalSeminarsTraining.com